Blueprints
To
Union

∞

BROTHER DOMINICK

DEDICATION

This book of Blueprints to Union is dedicated to the Beingness of God's Holy Union, The Holy Spirit, and Christ himself as an appearance and manifestation of God's Omnipresence. I would like to thank all the Monks and Hermits who have guided me along my travels and retreats while having been traversing my own undoing into Union, with an Emphasis on my correspondence with John the Hermit from South Africa. May this be the fruition of that which was promised to be done in pre-existence, the hearts promise in Union for the fulfillment of the Truth to bare itself experientially in transcendence and timelessness in those whom are called from the beginning of time. To my Sister whom I love dearly, may Union manifest in you in all its glory eventually. And to my Mother who is Joy and Love personalized, I look forward to your re-Union as well. Love is Omnipresent!

CONTENTS

Acknowledgments   I

Introduction   Pg 1

1   Michael's Exchange   Pg 5

2   Adam's Exchange   Pg 29

3   Hayley's Exchange   Pg 61

4   Emma's Exchange   Pg 77

5   Christina's Exchange   Pg 113

6   Questions & Answers   Pg 131

7   About the Author   Pg 161

ACKNOWLEDGEMENTS

As is true on the road to Union, where everything starts to be seen as happening on its own with no 'You' in it anywhere, this book took shape, formed, and came to life all in its own. It was in the unfoldment of selflessly sharing the process with others, that the same Union would be made revealed in them as it was in me, and as that mysterious evolution continued, it gave birth to this book, and a manifestation of something out of what once was, nothing. I'd like to thank Michael, Adam, Hayley, Emma, and Chris for giving me permission to share correspondences initially deemed private. By making them public and sharing the process with the world, we trust in Union that countless others will benefit from these beautiful life changing exchanges that lead to Union/Theosis/Deification.

INTRODUCTION

The following exchanges are a set of correspondences that took place with five different individuals over a course of 5 years that lead to each of them being able to experience Union with God(Theosis/Deification), to various degrees. An additional Q & A section will help to explain and shed light on some of the subtle intricacies and hang ups that can happen as a person is working out their way into the manifestation of the Union experience.

The purpose of these exchanges is for the reader is to understand them intellectually, to intuit what is being said, to feel it, to play with it like a child, and most importantly to start to apply these same teachings to your own experience so that over time, the Union experience will manifest in your own reality as well.

It is highly suggested to read and re-read these exchanges at different times in your life, as intellect, understanding, love, intuition, and your entire being can grow over time and reach new levels of higher understanding at later life periods to allow for a deepening of the wisdom and faculties that come with Union. Many times, people who I have shared these exchanges with really couldn't grasp them until some later time when it all fully sinks in, while still, others get it right away. It truly is all grace, blessings, and just allowing this whole process to take place, deeply sink in, and for Union to start to manifest of its own accord when the proper 'getting out of the way for it to happen,' is in place.

***

Along with these exchanges, it is highly recommended that the reader visit the YouTube channel here:

https://www.youtube.com/user/snbeings

And start to apply the following meditations:

30-60 Minutes daily, along with applying any time there is free time, driving, work breaks, etc:

https://www.youtube.com/watch?v=-N6uNS3XQtc

First 15-20 minutes upon waking up in the morning:

https://www.youtube.com/watch?v=xF_epqmv3_Q

Last 15-20 minutes just prior to falling asleep:

https://www.youtube.com/watch?v=EcpKdm7F464

Any questions (Q & A session/ Exchange) can be sent to Brother Dominick at: snbeings@gmail.com

This book is intended for those in whom the longing for Union with God is born, a longing in the heart that can only be quenched by Union itself and only the inner calling for Union is what can be met with the answer of Union itself.

Different individuals are in different places in their walk with God. From beginners who are just starting out, to intermediates who are still working through various stages of awakening, purifications, calling on Christ, Scripture study, and finally to those who have reached the maturity to go beyond words, beyond concepts, in whom that inner Union calling has been born like a newborn child, in the heart . It is for the latter group of people that these instructions are intended and it is only to those for whom this will be clear as the sky.

The instructions themselves are self filtering, since for the beginner, they will be completely above their head. And for the intermediate, they will be in too much doubt and ego based ignorance to give up either the old ego, or too wrapped up in the replaced religious based ego, in order to proceed.

I know this because it happened to me, as a beginner none of this would have made any sense, and as an intermediate there was too much of a comfort zone in the known religiosity with which I propped myself up. But after receiving the mystical graces of divine mercy and being slain by the Spirit, the inner path would be made known, and a Hermit would teach me the rest for Union to manifest, which is now being made known to you as the Blueprints to Union. It was only in maturity of Spirit and the birth of the heart's inner longing for Union, that the Blueprints could be understood and Union made manifest.

The following teachings that are revealed in this manual are introduced to the reader through the context of exchanges with others. It is therefore up to the reader, to extract what is being conveyed in the following text, and to apply said teachings to one's own apparent self in a manner the consists of specific contemplation, meditations, and cultivation.

Union with God is already everywhere, within everything, and the access to this reality is already there, within you, a Spiritual organ waiting to be awakened so it can see its inherent Union. It merely needs to be tapped into and accessed in a certain way, a specific way of seeing through the unreality of the ego and allowing for there to be a genuine and utter surrender and unknowing of all things. It is this embarking along a journey where you give up yourself, in exchange for Union with God.

This process is something that first and foremost has to be understood before it can be cultivated. That understanding comes from the direct application to one's self from the exchanges, following the meditations, through direct experience of one's reality, and through the undoing of all the identities that the ego/body believes itself to be.

A certain sense of entering into a Minimalistic period also helps, as it tends to unclutter the identity driven actions that are taken throughout the day, actions which help to avoid facing and figuring out the truth of the illusion of the ego. Since this is a process of seeing, undoing, and unraveling for Union to be revealed, then one's outer reality should also reflect what's going on within. It's the ultimate fasting, but it's fasting from thought, from all identifications, from the body, and anything that is considered to be 'you.'

This requires a certain daily to weekly self inventory check. Beside the basic necessities of your current life of sleep, work, cooking/eating, cleaning, bathing, and so on, we also fill our lives with time wasters which keeps us locked in the Egoic mode of status quo life. Internet, social media, texting, TV/Movies, videogames, books, seeking more knowledge and information, and other time wasters should be minimized and replaced with meditation, walks, contemplation, watching the ego, and applying all the teachings presented here forth. Once a certain intermediary experience and understanding of these teachings is in place, then those initial time wasters can be transformed into No Self Atmosphere cultivation practices which enhance and help Union to manifest eventually.

***

CHAPTER 1

MICHAEL'S EXCHANGE

As with most people, Michael came across my YouTube videos and contacted me through e-mail. He had gone through and graduated Seminary schooling in the southern part of the United States and had a Doctorate in Theology. It was initially an intuitive pull for him that if he was to fill himself up with scripture, opinions, theories, and the written word, that it would bring him closer to God. But upon graduating, he realized that though his head filled with so much knowledge, his heart still longed for direct experience, to truly know God. He had achieved many breakthroughs and eventually realized through direct experience the point of these teachings.

With Michael, I was still early in constructing a set of Blueprints that carried a variety of keys to help unlock Union. As I was still primarily focused on Seeing the Illusion of the Ego and Surrender from the center of Seeing/Awareness, it was still enough to produce the first glimpse into Union. Eventually I would go into additional key points and set up the Atmosphere of No Self Meditations along with the Am/Pm Meditations, but with Michael, it was simple and direct, and it worked!

Michael: Brother, your videos really struck a chord with me and I wanted to know if you can help me with Union. I have a Doctorate in Theology and initially joined because I always thought learning the Bible will lead me to God, and here I am years later knowing all these things, but lacking the direct experiences you speak of. I can feel you speak a genuine heartfelt truth and I would like to find out what you know. Can you work with me?

Dom: Greetings Brother, sure I can work with you and thank you for responding. I typically answer e-mails once a week or so for the purpose of you being able to really marinate with the teachings so that they fully sink in. We can Skype every so often and I do retreats once or twice a year as well, so there's always that.

As for your background, I think you heard in some of my videos my experiences with the leaders of churches, theologians, and various leaders of different denominations after having my initial Holy Spirit indwelling experiences in that, none of them really knew of the experiential ego death and ensuing stages/experiences that happen after that. I say this because of your background as a theologian, you can have your mind too filled with concepts and ideas of God, and yet don't or won't ever have the Union experience at all, and that's what I'm here for, a sort of midwife or finger pointer for your own access to Union. I must say, you have to let go of all this accumulated knowledge because Union is simple, it's about seeing through illusions and projections, especially the ones you have about yourself, then it becomes easy to surrender and for Grace to open access to Union. Luke 17:21 Christ says, "…..behold, the kingdom of heaven is within you." So you just have to look the right way for this to be revealed.

Michael: Okay, I think I understand. You're saying too much knowledge can be a stumbling block to experiencing God and I have to let go of all of this so I can look within, is this right? I don't really know where to look though, isn't God somewhere far away up there in the heavens and because we are sinners, we need to go through the whole liturgical process of redemption?

Dom: God is Omnipresent and everywhere all at once by his very nature if you even want to say "he" in the first place, because God transcends genders, labels, concepts.

Let me ask you something because there is a lesson here. If I told you that you can witness one of the most beautiful sunsets in your life that is specifically unique to the shores of Portugal in late August. The sun just seems so big during this time as the westerly winds brush across your face gently enough to cool you down after the adventures of the day. So after you have heard this minor description of a sunset if Portugal, have you imagined it?

Michael: Yes, I can imagine what it is like and have even added additional details like the beach, color of the sand, other tourists and so on.

Dom: Okay great! So you have constructed in your mind an imagined daydream of what it's like, and yet what you have constructed in your mind, is it the same as actually standing there on that beach in person and experiencing it directly?

Michael: No of course not. In my mind it's an unreal daydream, but the beach is actual.

Dom: Okay good, so you're telling me that if I gave you the choice and said, "Michael, would you rather have a round trip ticket to experience the sunset in Portugal, or experience it only in your own mind," which would you chose?

Michael: Of course I would want the actual ticket to experience the actual beach directly for myself.

Dom: Okay, perfect so you're with me up to this point. How about, would you rather have an actual million dollars of cash in a duffle bag given to you to do with whatever you please, or would you rather just have an imagined million dollars in your own mind to do with whatever you please? Also, please tell me why your choice is as it is.

Michael: I would pick the actual million dollars because it's real, whereas what is imagined is not real and therefore not usable in real life.

Dom: Okay, perfect. So do you understand thoroughly this point that what you have created in your mind isn't real?

Michael: Well, yes I understand, but thoughts I think are still real are they not? Aren't they representations like the language of the mind's eye or some sort of immaterial substance?

Dom: I really want to keep this simple so you get this point, so I want to stay on track with this because we can digress into branches of thought that is philosophical, neurological, theoretical, and so forth and literally discuss the topic of thought for hours or days on end as is done by academia. However, this is something else and I really want you to see this so I will ask again, is the thought of something the same as that actual something?

Michael: Well, no it's not.

Dom: So you agree that the thought of a million dollars is just a daydream and is not the same as an actual million dollars? The thought of a Portuguese sunset is just an imagined daydream and is not the same as the direct experience of standing there physically and experiencing the sunset?

Michael: Yes, I agree and I see your point. The differences between the two are clear.

Dom: Okay, so let's take this idea into your theological fields first. Do you have an imagined idea of what God himself is like, without any of the theological forms as Holy Spirit or Jesus, but the Godhead himself?

Michael: I mean sure I have some thoughts and ideas of what God is like and whatnot, but various theological studies discuss God being unfathomable. Is this what you are getting at, something like trying to fathom the size of space itself?

Dom: Yes, this applies to my former points. Do you see that whatever imagined ideas and constructs you have about God, are entirely imagined and limited? Do you see that they are just daydreams and illusions?

Michael: Yes, I see this and get your point. So no matter what I think, it's not the same as the actual thing. So God exists, but is nothing like what I think he is?

Dom: Exactly, and you can take it another step beyond that and start looking at all the thought based illusions your mind creates, many of which have no weight in reality at all, like with the future. Notice how there is no future because there is only really this present moment right now, and the future is just the mind playing with possibilities of what will be, and most times what eventual Is, is never like what the mind imagined it to be.

Michael: Okay yes, I see this and kind of feel now for the sake of discussion that maybe my schooling was for nothing, because I really went into thinking I would know God by learning so much Seminary knowledge and you are saying all of that is just daydreams?

Dom: Not quite. Knowledge is good to a point because you need to know the rules of driving to successfully get from A to B safely and you've established in your intellect a rich inner library of ideas about God that can be useful for the future, however I will quote the theologian Thomas Aquinas who wrote massive volumes of materials and eventually received a direct experience, possibly of Union, who said this: "The end of my labors has come. All that I have written appears to be as so much straw after the things that have been revealed to me. I can write no more. I have seen things that make my writings like straw."

You see how the direct experiences of God are beyond words, thoughts, concepts, daydreams and imagined illusions?

Michael: Yes, okay all of this logically makes sense, so how do I access this sort of experience?

Dom: There are several ways but I will show you the simplest and the easiest because many of the others are incredibly difficult struggles that most people today cannot even do. But first I want to now point out what you just said. You're asking how can you experience this for yourself yes?

Michael: Yes

Dom: So let's apply all those points we just discussed directly to you. Who do you think you are? Do you think you are this 'I' and can show you me this 'I' and put it in my hand? Check for yourself if this 'I' is real.

Michael: I think I'm a person, a male, a Christian and Theologian with various attributes both physical and psychological. As far as the 'I', it's a word I guess I can say, like a universal self reference.

Dom: Just like the unreal imagined Portuguese sunset, the unreal imagined million dollars, and the unreal imagined God, who you imagine yourself to be, is also unreal and imagined.

Michael: Okay this is interesting and it's rather philosophical but it seems like we are reaching again something unfathomable with all of this, are we not? It feels like we are treading into some sort of unknowingness, perhaps like the book, The Cloud of Unknowing.

Dom: You're jumping ahead Michael, just stay with me on this one because the secret to really unlock all of what I'm saying here in all of this is 'Seeing.' If you can clearly 'See' and do so regularly as a sort of meditation throughout the day, then you will be able to experience some of these things we have been talking about. You are now to cultivate, 'Seeing' the illusions and daydreams that the mind creates, and no longer identify with them, 'Seeing' that they aren't even real.

Again do you see when your mind references itself as the word 'I'? And can you tell me if this 'I' is real or an unreal imagined illusion? Take your time with this and be honest and genuine with all of this. Write back whenever you want or we can Skype another time as well. Just write back after wrestling with this for a day or two.

Michael: Okay, yeah you're right about this whole thing. The 'I' which I use as a self reference thought, is imagined and is unreal. I really tried to find any way possibly I could to debate this and philosophically argue against this point, but the more I sat and looked, the more I saw what you're pointing to.

I seem to self reference myself as this 'I' which is like an ongoing illusion for the sake of navigating reality right, but it doesn't end there upon investigation because at this point, any thought that you have about anything can than technically fall into this category of imagined or daydreamed illusions.

I mean, I am still this body and I am referencing it as me because it is different from other bodies and for the sake of communication. This is some profound stuff.

Dom: Okay, yes you are doing good so far, starting to investigate what is real, what is not real, and spending time Seeing, looking at things. Are you really the body though? We have among us paraplegics and various war veterans or victims of accidents who have lost limbs and yet are they still human and who can say what constitutes a whole full human?

Now even though I asked you that, see that any answer will be formulated as an imagined and daydreaming based response, so can we really say that response is true considering different people will respond differently? The answers amongst paraplegics themselves, is different as well, so who's really right? But again, let's not diverge off topic too much because this is mostly about you.

So let me ask you this. Is whatever you think about yourself, as unreal as daydreams of a million dollars, daydreams of God, and daydreams of sunsets in Portugal? And do you clearly see this in your own experience? Or is this just an intellectual understanding you have of this?

Michael: I mean, yes I see your point about all of this and it feels like the intellectual understanding of this is being formed through experience and investigation, just by really wrestling with this like you said.

Dom: Okay, good. So the first step is to really grasp this as an intellectual understanding but you are at a dead end if you stop there and this is really where some people I have worked with have a problem. They reach an intellectual understanding, but it isn't experiential and it absolutely has to be experiential for there to be some success with this, understood? So what I want you to do next is spend a few days really experiencing this. Remember, 'Seeing' this in your own experience is the master key and goes beyond just an intellectual understanding. So in your daily routines, watch how there is a daydreaming illusion playing out before you that is centered around this thought 'I'.

If hunger arises, there is an imagined daydream that says, "I am hungry and need to eat." But if we dissect this further on a physiological level and ask a doctor what is going on in terms of physical reality, he/she will explain to you that because of lack of food and a decrease in calories for energy use, there is a fluctuation of hormones (leptin/ghrelin) and this triggers hunger pangs which include the stomach growling, a physical feeling of having an empty stomach, and ultimately a feeling arises along these different factors of getting you to eat.

Technically, we can say the stomach is hungry and needs food in it. And yet, the imagined illusion is that this 'I' thought arises and superimposes itself over the stomach saying I need to eat. Clearly you aren't the stomach however, since there are plenty of medical cases annually of people who have various medical devices(feeding tubes/bags) that have replaced their missing stomachs due to illness or accidents.

Also, the body will age and die one day, and furthermore you can check for yourself. Ask yourself if you are your stomach. Really feel it and examine this question.

Do you understand so far what I'm saying?

Michael: Yes I understand, so you're saying to sort of watch what I label and how I label it and to examine the bodies needs and feelings along with how I label these feelings?

Dom: Yes, exactly, except with the added caveat that you see whatever label that is currently there, as just an illusion, an unreal daydream that's the same as the imagined million dollars and the imagined sunset.

Michael: Okay, so do I also apply this to other facets of my daily life?

Dom: To every facet of life. Remember the hunger pangs? What happens when the bladder is full?

Michael: I have to relieve myself.

Dom: Wrong! Answer with the introspection and change of perspective we just discussed using the stomach principal. Examine and break down what's really happening and tell me right now what is found.

Michael: Okay. So the bladder gets filled from the intake of fluids, it feels full, and needs to be released?

Dom: Yes, exactly! So the mind creates this unreal imagined illusion and says, "I have to pee." But really it's the bladder itself which needs to release excess fluid.

Michael: But how can I live like that? It seems like subtracting the 'I' out of everything would make it difficult to function.

Dom: You're starting to reach some vitally important conclusions intellectually, which is a good sign that all of this is sinking in, however your conclusion is incorrect. The stomach gets hungry, eating eventually happens, and urination happens automatically without needing to think about whether or not you are doing it. It just happens on its out and out of habitual tendencies.

Also, I'm not asking you to subtract 'I' out of anything, because then technically, you are implying there is an initial 'I' that is subtracting the 'I', creating a vicious cycle of illusion that is entirely unnecessary.

I'm asking you to 'See – Experientially' throughout the day in your daily routine, that the thought 'I' is just an imagined daydream like the sunset and million bucks, and realize it's not real whenever it arises. Consider it an ongoing thing throughout the day for a couple days and get back to me after telling me what remains 'Seen' through this process.

Note * (About a week later, Michael writes back)

Michael: Dom, I had a real intense dream last night after applying these instructions for the past week. I will admit I forgot to do it a lot, if not most of the time, but still I had plenty of breaks throughout days at work and on the weekend I spent some time really examining all of this a lot more and started following your meditation instructions on YouTube.

Anyway, last night I had a dream I was walking somewhere along a path in a park and eventually all the parts of the park begin to separate from each other, so instead of a whole park, it was dissecting slowly into a myriad of pieces. Before me was a huge spacious chasm that just appeared out of nowhere that I was beginning to fall down into, it was almost magnetic in its pull and I was getting sucked in but got scared and tried to fight my way out of there until I finally woke up.

When I woke up, my mind, I mean the state I was in was very vivid and lucid and it was impossible to fall back asleep again. I feel it's strongly connected to the practices you've given me and I'm not sure what to do next, but I haven't slept since then and finally decided to write you.

Dom: Michael, it's a good sign that the practice is starting to head in the right direction. The dream is also a sign that you need to learn the second master key and that is the proper form of surrender and we'll get to that because there is a right surrender and various wrong ones.

Tell me do you see in your direct experience now that the thought 'I' is a daydream, that it's unreal and an illusion? Do you see how anything that's thought, even the thinker of thoughts, all of it is all imagined daydreams?

Michael: Yes, I see it clearly. It's actually funny to me now to reference to myself as I, it feels kind of phony and humorous at the same time. It seems things are very light and there's a breeze to my step if that means anything.

I also noticed that if the 'Seeing' is not there, then all these thoughts in the forms of daydreams overtake me completely, whereas when 'seeing' is in place, things are a lot more calm and centered. Many times I won't catch it until I've already slipped into this active daydreaming. I seem to catch it much later in the day or 10-20 minutes after getting wrapped into a train of thoughts.

So this is very interesting and things feel and seem different, but I don't understand how this could lead to Union. Can you explain or at least give me some technical breakdowns or more details of how this all works because I'm very curious and intrigued with this.

Dom: Okay, so it's not you that's intrigued with all of this and not you that wants technical breakdowns, but it's this illusion and imagined 'I' that is looking for things to continue to perpetuate itself. This false 'I' with all of its wants and needs is what blocks Union from being revealed, and that chasm in the dream state was an opening into Union. However, the 'I' in the dream state attached itself to fear in order to continue to perpetuate itself in that state, hence why we will have to eventually discuss the proper form of surrender and letting go so that falling and surrender into the chasm of the unknown can happen.

There is the technicality that false 'I' wanted. Do you see how intricately crafted this whole mechanism is, how it attaches to wants, to needs, to emotions, to various patterns and habitual tendencies? And yet this 'I' itself is just a daydreamt illusion, a figment of imagination, a façade and it holds no reality just like the imagined million dollars and the sunset. Do you see?

Michael: Yes, wow you're completely right. All the games it plays and now I see in retrospect from the past week how many excuses came up and I even got angry in traffic for no reason because I was early to work anyway.

And regret too. I mean I can't go back and change things from the past that have already happened. Wow, you can probably write a book about all the things this 'I' thought does.

Dom: Ha! Yeah, you're preaching to the choir brother. So I want you now to spend a few days really deeply "Seeing'(as in being vividly aware of) all these things play out that revolve around the 'I' and how they are all daydreamt illusions. This 'Seeing' has to be established as a permanent feature so that it can see all the games and details this 'I'- thought plays out and most importantly, every time it's seen, right away it should be seen as the false daydream dancing about, playing out all of its different games, or whatever is revolving around it at the time that it's seen.

Now here's the next step and caveat of the practice. Every time that this 'I' is seen, or even if it's not the 'I' but many times it will be plans about the future, opinions of what a coworker said, ideas on what to eat for dinner, no matter what stream of thoughts are arising, see that it's an unreal daydream and surrender right there on the spot from this place of 'Seeing.' Understood?

Michael: Yes I understand everything except surrender. How is this done?

Dom: It takes practice to be understood experientially, or else you create a straw man of illusion of what it is. Surrender has to be first and foremost from this place of 'Seeing.' So whenever Seeing is in place, and whatever is seen as illusion in that moment, that illusion/daydream can be let go of and surrendered as not real so that 'Seeing' is simply in this surrendered state and resting in itself.

A not-so-famous quote by St. Francis of Assisi which has almost always been oft misunderstood is the following. "What we are looking for, is what is looking."

It is this 'Seeing/Seer' which has the ability to 'See' the illusion based unreality of the ego, which is what we are to See so that this Seer or Seeing is resting in itself, unidentified from anything else.

So even physically there can be a corresponding sigh of relief that goes on with this, a deep exhale, and a loosening of the whole body to correspond with the surrendering of each moment the illusion is noticed.

15

You already surrender all illusion and the entire body each night when you go to sleep, but you just weren't 'Seeing' how this surrender into sleep was happening, so now you have an additional assignment on top of learning to surrender, which is to bring 'Seeing' into the last conscious moment before sleep happens, understood? That way the surrender that happens into sleep each night becomes a teacher with an important lesson. This is what the P.M. Meditation is all about, to allow a conscious understanding of how surrender happens each night, and to allow sleep to happen in a non-clinging, non-grasping, non-identified with anything, state of the 'Seeing/Awareness' resting and surrendering in itself.

Michael: Okay yeah I think I got it. Just now as I was reading this, I noticed the thought and opinions that are centered around the 'I' daydream, want to interject and want to question more and certain junctions of reading the description. Instead, there was just a watching of this mechanism at play via the 'Seeing' practice as you describe, and then an immediate loosening of any physical tension and a deep sigh/exhale. Soon as that happened, all the questions and needs/wants to ask more seemed to disappear and everything was just still while I continued to re-read the instructions. Seems simple, like something that I can pick up with a few days practice, plus the mediations are really great to go deeper into all of this.

Dom: Yes this is good, and I know we are using language to communicate, but notice the whole last part of the last sentence in which you are referring to this all as something 'I' can pick up. Just make sure these sorts of patterns are seen as daydreams and illusions and are surrendered accordingly. So instead of 'I' am getting deeper into all of this, it's more so 'deeper' is happening all on its own without 'I'.

Also, the level of acquired surrender has to reach the point of being able to surrender life itself, to a point where if you were in the dream scenario again, and the chasm was to open back up, pulling you into it, that you would be able to surrender the 'I' and its attachment to fear, in order to accept completely this surrender into the chasm, understand the level that surrender has to reach.

And I will also add this here: Matthew 10:39 "He that findeth his life shall lose it; and he that loseth his life for my sake shall find it."

I will ask in all seriousness, do you understand the proximity and level of surrender that has to take place? It means a surrender even if it's at the cost of your own existence, complete, thorough, full, and 100% genuine, capiche?

Michael: Yeah, wow this very serious stuff. You know I will admit when I first found your videos and contacted you, it seems like on an unconscious level I was just collecting more knowledge of various sorts and yours seemed exotic, like it would cost something for me to get it, just like all my loans to pay for Seminary.

Even saying all of this, or rather typing all of this, the 'Seeing' you mention is in place and I 'See' the words and structures as they are formulated before they are typed out. I'm going to allow all of this to be surrendered now and do as told.

Yeah, there is a stillness and peace there now, and the Seeing is very vivid and alive in the midst of everything. I'm going to give it all another go and will get back.

Note * After that and as usual with the majority of contacts, Michael disappeared for a month and I hadn't heard from him, but knew intuitively that a seed had been planted and that quite possibly the Seed of Seeing/Awareness was planted. One day there was an intuitive feeling within about Michael, and later that day there was an e-mail from him to see if we can chat over the phone for a bit.

Michael: Something happened to me, or rather something happened and I can't explain it. I was hoping to get your take on it. I took your instructions and printed them out, re-reading them daily while making it a habit to keep this Seeing/Surrendering deal going and I brought Seeing into the process of falling asleep as well like in the P.M. Meditation on YouTube. Some days I skipped, don't know why exactly because after a while of doing this, there is no skipping and the Seeing process you refer to keeps going, taking on a sort of life on its own.

Well those days that I chose not do any of this, I found myself again wrapped up in the 'I' and all of its dramas, complaints, issues, and so forth and it's actually really unpleasant to live that way to be quite honest.

Dom: Yeah, this is all good. These are intuitive truths becoming revealed as direct experiences.

Michael: Okay, yeah I can see that. Anyway, so realizing how unpleasant that 'I' is, I reverted, sometimes automatically, into the Seeing/Surrendering mode of being, and the live daydream apparatus, as I've kind of coined it, just eases up and becomes a lot less still and calm and it's actually a preferred way of being.

Dom: Yeah, again that's all intuitive insight arising there. Just need the process to keep building up steam, keep it going with the cultivation of all of this daily.

Michael: Yeah, I see the trend with this clearly, but here's what eventually happened. I'm driving home from work and the 'Seeing' is very vivid and in one moment I catch the 'I' thought before it was about to wrap itself into a complaint about the traffic right? And then I see this 'I', clear as day, wanting to attach to the next string of complaints and can see what it's about to be before it even has the chance to construct itself, it was going to be something like, "it doesn't matter if you caught me and see me anyway, you're still stuck in crappy traffic."

Only instead of the mind saying that, the vividness of the Seeing ability stopped it in its tracks from even going down that train of thought. And then like in rapid succession, no matter what was about to be thought or projected via this daydream apparatus, everything was being seen through and surrendered calmly, while still having eyes on the road enough to drive safely.

Dom: Yes, another good sign post along the way.

Michael: Good, so it sounds like you're familiar with what happens. Anyway, my Seeing is just on a roll now, getting better and brighter daily.

Dom: I just wanted to add something in there if I may. Can you have this 'Seeing' happening on its own like we discussed the stomach being hungry and the bladder needing to pee, and yet both of these aren't you, so can you apply this to 'Seeing' itself? As in, Seeing is happening on its own, without a Seer.

Michael: (He laughs when I ask him this before continuing) Yes, I believe you've read the 'I's' mind because this is where I'm going next. So with the constant seeing though all daydreaming, eventually of course the traffic clears up, and I make my way home while still in this state. So I stop at the last stop sign before turning, and look both ways when it happened.

Dom: What happened?

Michael: It's like I disconnected from the mind, I mean, not I disconnected but Seeing itself disconnected from the mind and I was watching/seeing this whole mechanism unhinged before me as it desperately looked for a place to latch back onto?

Dom: Yes I know this stage. It's basically the nonstick state of Seeing, where the ego/mind has nothing to stick to. The ego illusion becomes loosened and unhinged from its ability to imprison the faculty of 'Seeing/Awareness,' and so it acts out in various ways. Did the surrender continue?

Michael: Wait can you repeat what you just said?

Dom: Yeah, I see this all as the faculty of Seeing/Awareness being imprisoned by the daydreaming/egotism falsehood. I mean, it's just a belief, an imagination itself, however if this isn't seen then the majority of people continue to live first of all with zero access to Union, and second of all entirely imprisoned by this illusion machine which they take to be not only real, but they believe it is who they are.

Michael: Yes exactly like in my experience. So here I am, Seeing, completely freed from the 'I' thought, actually from the entire thinking structure I saw how this thinker of thoughts isn't who I am and the thinking process is going crazy trying to get the faculty of Seeing to wrap back up in its story lines.

Dom: Did surrender continue?

Michael: No it didn't. I was just fascinated by what had happened and got wrapped up in writing this long 10 page e-mail worth of insights when you didn't pick the phone that day. And I was being shown all these psychological patterns that got picked up from childhood and different aspects of the mind. I was just in awe and became hyperactive by what had happened. It was like the first time I ever really felt a burden had lifted and like I was free as bird. But to make a long story shorter, I went to sleep that night and when I woke up the next day, everything was intact just like before, the 'I' and all its daydreams where there in place from the very first onset of awakening in the morning.

So now I'm wondering was I on the right track and how do I get back to that?

Dom: You were on the right track and that was a very vital and important step, however the lack of continual surrender sabotaged a further progression. Also you can't get that back, because that implies an 'I' which has to do something in order to re-experience something like that, when in reality that was Grace.

A moment of Grace like that can return again as long as there is a continual seeing that the thought process isn't real, that it isn't who you are, and that it's a daydream that isn't getting wrapped up in, but most importantly there has to be non-stop and continual surrender.

The mind/ego illusion tricked you up by the fascination of the experiencing, the need of the mind to write 10 pages, to call me that day, and the lack of continuing to surrender and let go of whatever it produces to the Seeing faculty, understand?

Michael: Yeah, I think so. It sort of felt like I opened access to a deeper portion of the illusion, things I've never seen before.

Dom: Yeah, that's what happens, the subconscious starts to release various things like fear or fascination or a multitude of ideas and emotions in order to reattach and imprison the Seeing(perceiving within) faculty. The only way to continue forward is when that ever happens again, even if it's in a dream state, is a continual surrender without wrapping up in any fears, fascinations, surprises, and so forth. Some people sometimes have spontaneous needs to cry or shout or in my case go for a 3 hour drive to nowhere in fascination while laughing to myself about the matter.

So in those kinds of situations, you sort of have to let out and appease whatever is arising at that point as a sort of letting go of subconscious baggage and patterns, and of course that's also part of surrendering to whatever needs to be communicated or rather released from the depths.

Cool, so there was a minor revelation of the possibilities and kind of an introduction to the inner subtleties, and sometimes not so subtle, inner realms of trying to locate the kingdom of God within you, except you are only allowed to enter when there is no more you, understood? When that belief in a separate 'you' is no longer believed in, then the illusion of this false identity starts to loosen and become unglued or unhinged, which will give birth to access to Union via surrendered non-clinging, non-grasping, disidentified letting go of all things and identities.

Michael: So what's supposed to happen is the perceiving faculty detaches from the daydream imprisonment and then leaves the body to go merge with God? Things aren't too clear there for me, and at one point when I was wondering, or rather when the mind mechanism was entertaining scenarios on what is next, there was a bit of fear that arose there.

Dom: No, you're jumping ahead of things. Perception as a form of consciousness can, under certain circumstances, leave the body and have various spiritual realm experiences, and that does manifest as a spiritual gift in some of the people I work with, however this is something else. The surrender is what opens up Union and the surrender is more like a vertical dropping down into a chasm, that chasm is the entrance into the Spiritual Heart, the portal to Union.

Remember your dream?

Michael: Yeah.

Dom: If you would have surrendered right then and there and let go of fear, that would have been the chasm to drop into, in order to enter Union. However, I don't want to say more or the 'I' has arsenal to project possibilities and perpetuate itself via false daydream constructs.

It's really quite simple. It's a combination of integrated Seeing/Perceiving of the Ego/Mind (I thought and everything it attaches too) as a false daydreamed illusion that isn't who you are, followed by a constant surrender/letting go of any experiences or phenomena that arise, including fear, fascination, the need to call me right away, and I mean

21

EVERYTHING has to be let go of, so its whole and thorough. This will loosen awareness from the headspace so that it can fall via surrender from the head and into the heart, where the portal to Union opens up.

It's not hard or difficult, because to say that it is so, is just another projected daydream construct of the ego/I-thought and hard/difficult doesn't exist as something real and tangible you could put in my hand for me to see, you see?

Michael: Yes it's all making sense now. Because of the lack of surrender, there was a re-imprisonment of the perception by the daydream faculty, right?

Dom: Yes, exactly. Even to say that, isn't true because it's just sort of something I made up as a way to communicate this. If you look closely, there is no 'I' that is imprisoned and there is no prison, because those two are just daydream based illusions and aren't real either.

But still it 'seems' that Perception/Seeing has to sort of regain its sovereignty and independence of being able to see clearly and without being clouded by daydreams in order for all of this open up.

Anyway Michael, I have to get going as I'm busy on some projects here at the house and I want you to step it up a bit. Keep this formula going so that it gains a decent amount of steam, and remember to continue letting go of/surrendering whatever the daydream machine produces, even if it's ecstasy, light, fear, crying, just be with whatever is arising, accepting that it is there, but not identifying with anything so that it remains clearly in the light of perception/seeing. Understood?

Michael: Yes, I got it. All of this is quite clear so I will spend some time with a print out of some notes I wrote down and previous e-mails and go over it a few times along with the practices, and get back to you when I have more to share.

I noticed, the ego construct does have a ton of theological questions about how this process ties into the things of Christ, and I know you already gave some verses in light of this, but it still feels like some pattern based on the theological schooling to pick your brain some more on these matters even though the practices have clearly bared some experiences.

Dom: It's a good thing the perception faculty sees all of this instead of identifies all of this. There's no reason to get into theological discussions and debates because you already got years of it that filled your head and no experience to show for it, as you admitted. Also, once you unravel the Union experience, everything just makes sense there, you'll see. Just keep applying what was said and get back to me after there is another extremely clear point that is reached in seeing that there is no 'I' and surrender happens.

This whole process is deeply rooted and established in the historic Eastern Orthodox Christians, Desert Fathers, Monks, Mystics, Hermits, and Saints within various Christian denominations of antiquity under the guise of the Theosis/Deification process. You can Google the following link for some background, but after it has been read, let it all go and return to the Seeing/Awareness resting in itself as we have been discussing in the surrendered state of disidentification of all things/identities.

https://en.wikipedia.org/wiki/Theosis_(Eastern_Orthodox_theology)

Note * It was a while before I heard from Michael again, as is common in my communications mostly because life beckons people to its ways. Between work, home construction projects, some car troubles, family, and all the other aspects of life that everyone is called to, there is very little time for people to focus solely on the Spiritual life. But Michael realized several insights during his time away.

Michael: Just wanted to check back in and share some more experiences with you, primarily the fact that when clear and present perception sees through the illusions of the mind, it really leaves you with some important qualities of stillness and peace, and just makes you more conscious of yourself. I was able to start integrating this practice into the my daily routine no matter what was happening, but found that I lost myself, or rather perception got wrapped back up in illusion a lot when talking to others.

So interacting with people became a weak point for me, but I kept at it and eventually arrived again at a separation of the ego from perception, only this time, after the initial excitement there was an immediate surrender like you spoke of, and just a consistent ongoing surrender of everything.

Well, the ego didn't like this one bit and tried all sorts of trickery and illusions to wrap itself back up into perception just like the first time. Luckily it was a Sunday and I had all day to really just be present with what was happening. So after an hour of sitting with all of this, everything just sort of fell away. I mean, there was no more thought, no more trickery, no more illusions, it's like the entire structure fell away and there was just clear and naked perception.

I really wasn't sure what to do next because there were no thoughts on what to do next. I suppose I could have sat there for days like that. Everything was just brighter and clearer, just really crystal clear. Well, eventually I suppose I got up but I don't know where the urge to get up came from or why, perhaps some unseen pattern, maybe something really subtle. Anyway, I was making my way to the kitchen and when I got there, even though I had been in there thousands of times, this time it was like I was really seeing it with newborn eyes, everything so fresh and clear, like for the first time in my life I can really see.

Now I knew I was having this experience, but I wasn't thinking because there were no thoughts, it was just some kind of directness about it, and it was unspeakable. So I poured a glass of water just enjoying this heightened and clear perception, and after turning off the water filter and sitting down at the table, I just completely disappeared. I really don't know what to say after that, but there really was no me anywhere to be found. I'm actually still quite speechless about it.

Dom: Yes, go into some details on the disappearance if you could explain it in the best way. Don't worry about word use, just be direct and let it out.

Michael: I mean there was no me anywhere. I disappeared but everything was still there, but it was all one thing. I guess I can say I lost all boundaries to myself and couldn't find where I was, it was really quite fascinating and yet, I had no way to think about what was going on because there was just that experience by itself, but there was no me to experience it because it was just a vast unity if I can call it that.

Even the sounds I heard from the closed window, some muffled birds chirping, a car passing, some of the neighbors kids riding past the house on their bikes, there were no boundaries in all of those sounds. There were no distinctions because the birds were not separate from the car or the kids, there really was no way they could be separate. Even now just thinking about it in retrospect of the experience, it's quite ridiculous to ever be able to see anything as separate again. I'm finding this quite difficult to verbalize so I apologize in advance for keeping it short.

Dom: You said "in retrospect,' so my next question is if there continues to be no 'you' anywhere to be found?

Michael: No the experience has passed. I mean, I can't even really call that an experience because it's still with me in some strange way days later and hasn't gone away. It seems like if I just relax a bit, especially when trying to fall asleep, the unity reappears. But the unity somehow isn't always there. Sometimes I am back in the experience of either perceiving in a heightened state, and other times the illusion daydream plays out its identities and perception is lost.

Dom: Can you tell me what happened in that primary unity, in the kitchen, where that was eventually lost?

Michael: I had some family come over that night for dinner and there were some things to prepare ahead of time that I agreed to help out with, but completely forgot to do because of the awe of the experience. All was lost when I opened the door to them.

Dom: (I pause to gently laugh at his description remembering my own integrations) Lol, yes of course, communication is a weak point that seems to give the flavor that there is a pulling out of Union. I understand. This stuff takes time to integrate and especially around the communication with others. You're in a good place though because you mentioned in many instances of relaxation, the Unity appears, which means the central channel to Union is now partially opened, requiring just a relaxed surrender for all things to come together again.

I think you see where this is headed next. The ability of integrating not just longer periods of stabilized Union, but also to be able to live from this Union and do all the things you normally do including interacting with people. Also, all the other practices still stand as well, so a continued cultivation of Seeing that the Illusions, particularly the 'I-Thought' isn't who you are so there is constant detachment from this mechanism until one day it becomes permanent. The thinker of thoughts, is an illusory daydream, a phantom which believes itself to be real when really it isn't.

Michael: That just sounds impossible. Can a person really live like that? When I was in Union, there was no time, no space, no anything, I mean everything was still there, but it's not like it usually was.

Dom: That's just the mind projecting and assuming ideas about something it doesn't know about and no it's not like that. Of course Union carries with it the sense of timelessness, even in my own experience I've had to keep clocks around and make a habit to check on them in order to keep appointments and promises, or else a day is just an hour or vice versa. So sure there will be some changes, but it's nowhere near some comatose state of being. Also, you've only experienced the Unity aspect of Union. There is much more to it than that. The Unity is also Love, it is also light, bliss, and many other facets that take time to manifest. All that to say that yes, you can live and function fully from Union.

Michael: I really want to thank you and you've been in my prayers and I have to say I have been permanently changed. I still have an inkling of sorts for discussing some more with you how Union all ties into my theological studies if you have something I can read, I would really appreciate it.

Dom: No problem, that's what I'm here for and I keep you in my prayers for Godspeed Union. As for a tie in, I'm writing some more in depth blueprints on how Union works and how it ties into the teachings of Christ, and I'll send you over some sample chapters when it comes together some more. Also, I can really easily distilled it with one verse in Jesus' prayer for us: John 17:21 "That they may all be ONE; as thou, Father, art in me, and I in thee, that they also may be ONE in us: that the world may believe that thou hast sent me.

Note * As is usual for most people I work with who reach this stage, it can really only go one of two ways; progression or stagnation and sometimes with a third possibility of teeter tottering between the two. In the following months I would check in with Michael and he would tell me he still had some access to Union but it was limited to certain occasions of deep surrender and had not been stabilized nor integrated. But he admitted he had been fundamentally changed from a very deep place within by the exchange and continues to put the teachings into practice.

This was also a time I realized that most people were playing out various egoic patterns of behavior even after a Union experience and that it was vitally necessary, like in my own experience, to really set aside some serious time for this to be seen and put into practice, especially in some sort of retreat setting where this is the only focus.

I had also at this point contemplated how the other traditions used other methodologies to help in the integration and stabilization stage of Union, and began to approach the people I was working with in a variety of ways after key insights were revealed. In Michael's case, as is important on this path, is that once he experienced Union, he always knew now with his whole being that everything really is One in God and that gave him some insights into interactions with others really not being interactions but like a play that the Oneness is putting on, almost pretending to be a variety of people all engaged in various acts he would later write.

But most importantly, seeing that the 'I-Thought' is a false construct and everything the daydreaming mind display's before perception is just a fantasy illusion, is something he can never unsee again. It was a permanent seeing and even if there was a slipping up back into any false identities, they had all lost their gusto of being anything real or permanent, making it easy to return to seeing/perceiving followed by surrender, and that in itself had changed his life(realizing there is no him) as he continues to extend experiences of Union(or rather Union extending itself) to longer integrated and stabilized degrees.

***

CHAPTER 2

ADAM'S EXCHANGE

Adam got a hold of me some time in 2013 at a time when the Blueprints were being sharpened by working with people locally, via e-mail exchanges, phone, Skype, and my own depths of unraveling into Union. As a busy college student with a part time job, a girlfriend, social media interactions, and a very busy and hectic schedule, he eventually realized that if he could just get a better understanding of the blueprints of these teachings, and formulate some sort of structure to each one of his busy days, that it would help his own unraveling into Union process.

It took a few months for everything to finally catch on with the help of the exchange below, along with reading and grasping some of the other initial unedited exchanges I started sharing with him from some of the other people who had traversed their way into Union. It would all eventually coalesce into a variety of signposts and insights that would eventually lead into Union itself.

Adam: Hey what's up Bro? Peace and all that good stuff. One of my Bible study buddies sent me over your stages to Union videos. He's pretty much the only other person I can discuss alternative views of Christianity with so I just wanted to show some love and respect for putting these views out there. Also, if you have anything else to share like some books or teachings that are more in depth on these stages, that would be cool if you could share for sure.

Dom: Thanks for the e-mail Adam. I've been doing these lengthy exchanges with people, which includes guidance via email exchanges and some practices to unravel Union. If you're all for it and 100% legit about being serious with this whole process, genuine, sincere, we can give it a shot

Adam: Yes for sure I'm serious and super interested. I have a real crazy schedule with school and all the other stuff going on, but there's just this inner hunger for the truth, I really have to take you up on the offer if you don't mind.

Dom: Alright, so I'm just going to get right to the point. Can you tell me what is this thought 'I', really look at it, and examine it throughout the day and tell me what you find. Be an investigator, or a detective, who is solving the case of this suspect called 'I'. Spend a day or two with this investigation, maybe take some notes whether mental notes or in a diary, and tell me what you find. Take some time to do it over a couple days or so to see if there are any patterns that this suspect keeps repeating.

Adam: Okay so I did as you said and found some interesting things. This thought 'I', is used to reference to myself, my point of view, my perspective, my body, everything that revolves around me. Especially when I'm talking to someone and in use of language, there really is no way out of using this word for sake of communication, for self reference. So if someone asks me what I did on my days off last weekend, I have to reference to myself using this thought and word called 'I'.

Dom: This is good, so you're starting to see what this 'I-Thought' is doing and that's the first step, just creating this habit of watching it and seeing what it does and all of its habits. So going further down this path of investigation, can you tell me what does this 'I' think it is?

Adam: A guy, 23 years old, engaged, a Christian, college student, enjoyer of different genres of music, kayaker, drummer, seeker of God, part time employee at the computer room on campus, also sort of a rebel against the traditional ways of seeing Christianity from the older generations, a philosopher, book reader, struggler with porn, rough childhood, there's honestly a lot there and I can probably write pages listing all the different things. Some seem good, some bad, some neutral and I can write down my whole history and background of how I grew up and all the things I've been through that have brought me to where I am today.

Dom: This is all good for now. We can get into the past maybe at a later point; because I want to specifically focus on this 'I' and what it thinks it is first, before going into more of the past. So let's take all those things and start dissecting them. What does that mean that you think you are a "guy"? Do you have to think that you are a guy, to be a guy? Or is the experience of being a guy happening all on its own?

Adam: Yes, of course the experience of being a guy is happening all on its own and no I don't have to think I'm a guy to be a guy.

Dom: Okay great! So you would agree that this experience and feeling of 'Guy-ness, male, manhood, etc' is all happening on its own right? Do you have to think "I am a Guy" for that to be so, or is thinking "I am a guy" something separate from the experience of being a guy?

Adam: Like I said, I don't have to think "I am a guy," to be one, it's just already something that is automatically there. Yeah its separate, being a guy is there all the time regardless of whether I think I am a guy or not. Or they can both be there, like the experience of being a guy is there and also the thought of being a guy can be there at the same time as the experience.

Dom: So let me get this straight, if the experience of being a guy is already there, and exists on its own, and doesn't require any thoughts about it for it to be as it is, then tell me which one is real. Is the direct experience of 'Guy-ness/Male-ness' the real thing, or are the thoughts of being a guy the real thing?

Adam: The experience is the real thing, and the thoughts are just ideas and I guess you can say representations in the mind about the experience.

Dom: So experience, being a guy, seeing, hearing, walking, breathing, everything that happens in experience, does that all happen regardless of what is thought about it? Do all those things require thoughts to exist, or do they all exist regardless of whether there is anything thought about them or not?

Adam: Yeah, you're right, it doesn't matter what's thought about those things because they already are as they are. I was just typing this reply and looking at the keyboard, but it was all sort of going on by itself and I didn't have to really think about my eyes for them to continue seeing the keyboard, it was just automatic.

Dom: So is the sense of seeing happening all on its own? Do eyes require any beliefs, or thoughts, or ideas or anything for them to be able to see, or do they see all on their own regardless of anything?

Adam: Man this is some crazy stuff! Honestly I can't believe I never questioned any of these things before. It's pretty strange, like if I put focus on my eyes, then it's like I perceive that they are seeing. But I usually don't do that, which means that they are just seeing on their own without me really putting any focus on them at all.

Dom: Can you tell me why you don't usually perceive that eyes are seeing? Where is perception usually going, perceiving? Don't answer right away, spend some time just examining your direct experience and tell me what you find after some time. Even just sitting there in one spot for 10 minutes should be a good preview.

Adam: Its thoughts, just nonstop thoughts about all sorts of things, like finding things to do, check my phone for texts, facebook, instagram, check what time the basketball game is on tonight, remembering things I still have to do today, double checking my schedule for the lab tomorrow, figuring out what to eat in a little bit, calling back my girl when we're done with the session, remembering something funny that happened yesterday.

Dom: When you perceived all that stuff, did you ever perceive, even once, that the eyes were seeing, or ears were hearing, or the present moment?

Adam: Nope, not at all, completely wrapped in all of those things, completely and fully consumed by them. This is crazy, how have I not seen this before? I think I see what you're getting at, we're so wrapped up in ourselves that we don't really take time to pause and be aware of all the other things?

Dom: Yeah that's just a small part of it. It's more so that all of those things the ego was doing, looking for things to do, to plan, to find, memories, etc, it's all a live daydream that isn't even real, and because of this live daydream, you are completely wrapped up in it and haven't yet snapped back into the reality of the present moment, and how it's all naked and prior to thought, but coincidentally can also include thought as well. So let me ask you if you've ever daydreamed in class & then snapped out of it, back into reality?

Adam: Yeah, of course.

Dom: Was the daydream real or an illusion?

Adam: It was an illusion but it produced some real physical consequences, especially the daydreams of a specific girl I had a crazy crush on freshman year who happened to be a senior. So it's kind of confusing because if it's an illusion, how could it produce a hard on (arousal)?

Dom: Was there an experience of the daydream that happened, and then after that, an experience of the physical ramifications of the daydream? Do you see that at the very root of whatever is happening, is that there is an experience of whatever is happening?

Adam: Yeah I think I got you, so you're saying that the experience I had was both of an unreal daydream and also of a real arousal, am I right?

Dom: You got it, but let's take this one step further. Did you once believe in Santa Claus when you were a little boy?

Adam: Of course!

Dom: Do you remember all the emotions, the heightened excitement, running to the tree in the morning to see all the gifts under it, and all the other real emotions and reacts to the gifts?

Adam: Yeah I remember and honestly wish I could go back to those days.

Dom: So would you say the reactions, emotions, excitement, the heightened energy, surprise, the gifts, the Christmas tree, parents, siblings, the whole experience and everything that was experienced was real?

Adam: Yes for sure all real, no doubt about it bro!

Dom: But there was a belief that some bearded guy named Santa Claus came and brought all these gifts, and the belief in Santa is a lie? A day dreamed illusion yes?

Adam: Ahhh okay, I see what you're saying. So all these reactions and emotions were real experiences but they were all based on the illusion of Santa. So the reactions of my physical body were all real that day in the classroom, but they were based on the daydream of my senior crush.

Dom: Exactly, you're getting it and these are good insights. What about the 23 years old thing? Is the thought, "I am 23 years old" real or not? Do you have to think "I am 23 years old" to be 23 years old, or is it also something that just exists all on its own?

Adam: Yeah, this is exactly like the first example. It just is what it is, regardless of what I think about it. Me communicating to you that I'm 23 years old is for you to get a better idea of me, I guess. The thought that I am 23 years old isn't the same as the experience of being that old.

Dom: Can you tell me if the experience of 'Being a guy' is the same as 'being 23 years old'?

Adam: Yeah this is crazy, it's like if I think about it, it's different than feeling about it. This is crazy strange! So if I feel what it's like to be a guy, it wasn't always like this. I was once a baby, then a boy, then puberty, then a man and in all those instances there was a different amount years old. And then into the future just judging on what happens to everyone else, there will be growing older, and more years added to the body. But this is an experience, and the thought of it isn't the same as the experience, is this right?

Dom: Yeah, this is good; it's just breaking down experience and seeing directly what's happening. So you went into the past and had ideas, memories, and concepts about the body in the past. Does that past exist currently or is it all just thought based, like day dreams? Same thing about projecting into the future, is that future here yet, and is the past already gone?

Adam: Yeah they're just thoughts and there is only right now as a direct experience.

34

Dom: Okay, so far so good. So are the thoughts 'I am a guy' and 'I am 23 years old' real or not. Are those thoughts real? Can you prove to me that these thoughts are real so I can see them? Can you put them in my hand so I can hold them and examine them? Is the experience of the body real or not?

Adam: I mean, these thoughts only exist in my own mind and no, I can't put them in your hand so you can examine them. The thoughts seem real to me and I don't know how I can prove to you that they're real. Experience of the body seems real too.

Dom: So those thoughts happening in your mind only happen in your own mind and in nobody else's right?

Adam: Of course

Dom: Is the thought 'I am a guy' different then that experience of 'Being a Guy'? Can you tell me what they are?

Adam: Yes, they are both experiences, but they are different. The experience of being a guy is a combination of things, a body with a penis, testosterone, deep voice, different senses like hearing and seeing, touch, moving around, there's a lot there. But the thought "I am a guy" is just thoughts.

Dom: So can the experience of being a guy, be there without the thoughts 'I am a guy?' Or does the thought 'I am a guy' have to be there in order for the experience of being a guy to be there also?

Adam: No, I don't have to think 'I am a guy' for that experience to be there. It's just always there, it's my default like we already discussed, and I get this part completely.

Dom: Is it your default or is it a default that doesn't belong to anyone? Is it just something that is happening on its own? Or do you have to do anything to make sure the default experience is in place?

Adam: Yeah, wow, this is pretty cool. So you're saying that being a guy is its own thing, and not necessarily my default? Is that even possible?

Dom: Investigate, see for yourself. There is the experience of being a guy, all by itself, happening automatically. Then some thoughts arise and say, 'this is my default.' Are these thoughts, 'this is my default' real? Or are they just imagined? Does the default of 'guy-ness/male-ness' require the thoughts 'this is my default' to be as it is, or does it exist on its own regardless of what thoughts are there about it, or not there about it?

Adam: Yeah you're right. It doesn't matter what I think about it, it's just there on its own as it is, regardless of what I claim about it.

Dom: So if it's true that being a guy is happening all on its own, and this experience doesn't need thoughts to be as it is, and that its default experience is different than the thoughts about it, can you get used to seeing it this way? The experience of the body is happening all on its own, it is its own default and it doesn't belong to any thoughts? Experiencing everything as happening all on its own.

Adam: So what you're saying is I am not the body? I'm confused here. I mean I understand completely what you're saying, and it's true, the default of this body does exist on its own regardless of what I think about it, but it still feels like me.

Dom: Is 'I' real or just a thought? Be serious, be 100% honest. Is the imagined thought of the tooth fairy real? Is the imagined thought 'I' real? Spend some time with this, you don't have to answer right away. Take a few days, take a week and really look at this thought 'I' and tell me if it's real, or if it's just being imagined.

Adam: Holy crap, this is crazy, I think I see what you're saying, haha, I mean even saying 'I' and referring to myself is strange now. Yeah, I think I get it. I'm definitely going to spend some time with this and get back to you in a bit. Thanks, for all this Dom, I can't believe I never really questioned my own experience and these things I thought about myself. Get back in bit, gotta get to class. Later!

Okay, so back from class. It was strange listening to the lecture and taking notes in class, I felt strange, almost out of body if you could call it that. I'm starting to just look at everything and re-examine my beliefs about my experience and it certainly is having some sort of effect on me that's out of the norm. Is this the grace you spoke of in some of the other exchanges?

Dom: Yeah it is. Questioning the ego, the body, the entire bias bubble of daydreams that is usually unexamined and unquestionably believed in, starts to bring about manifestations of grace and subtle changes that will start to unglue things, to pop the bias bubble eventually.

So do you see how the ego is just constantly producing nonstop daydreams about all sorts of things?

Adam: Yeah, I'm starting to see the thoughts constantly commenting on all sorts of things, but it only happens when I question it and make a conscious decision to check it out. If I don't do that, then I'm completely wrapped up in it, but that's just the last few hours and I honestly have no clue how you're going to resolve this with me, I'm probably the worst case scenario A.D.D., crazy busy with life stuff, I guess I just have doubts.

Dom: Those doubts are they real things that exist that everyone can experience objectively and realistically, or are they limited to a daydream that exists only in the ticker tape of illusions called your ego? Are these doubts about you in my ego also?

Adam: Yeah I think I'm catching it now and no they don't exist in your ego, at least I don't think they do.

Dom: Can you just drop them? Try it, see if you can just let go of doubts and let them fall away by no longer identifying with them. So instead of wrapping yourself up in this loop of thoughts that say, "I have doubts," can you just see the doubts as "doubts that are arising on their own but they aren't mine, or, "there doesn't have to be any identification with them as my doubts."

Adam: I mean they're already there and I'm already identified with them, but I see what you're saying. So next time something like this comes up, if I can catch it, I have a choice of whether or not I will identify with it right?

Dom: Exactly the point of the process. Get used to doing that, so that there is a habit of seeing everything that arises in the ego, emotions, body, and choosing to no longer identify with anything that arises. This alone done for X amount of time (that amount of time is different for each person) will eventually start to unglue the ego, and various subconscious things will start rising up to the surface, like a deep rooted fear in losing this ego, and that too has to be chosen to not be identified with. This deep rooted fear is usually one of the last vestiges blocking access to Union.

Adam: Yeah, I get this from the other exchanges, but it just seems like that's such a hard thing to do, to constantly catch all the thoughts arising and not identify with them.

Dom: Listen Adam, sometimes all it takes is a single moment of seeing this whole process as being a bunch of unreal daydreams and as not you, just one time, in the right circumstance, so that a domino effect begins and knocks down the rest of the imagined unreal dominos to be knocked down automatically.

So it's really just having a continuation of this that keeps going throughout the day. Naturally there will be a forgetting of this and a return into the live daydreaming of the ego, but creating this habit to see what it's doing, to see that it's all just imagined unreal daydreams, and to see that the whole daydream structure isn't who you are, will start an amazing process that will reveal grace, the ego will lose its glue, and there will be revealed an entrance into Union that is surrendered into.

The whole ego process is like this thief that's sneaking around in the house in the dark while you are sleeping. Because it's dark and because you are in deep sleep and having all these illusion based dreams, you're not aware of the thief. This thief was tricking you because you were sleeping, so he was pretending to be you by doing whatever he wanted in this house, watching TV, laughing, making jokes, having ideas, comments, opinions, projections, illusions, all out loud while you were sleeping. So the first step is to wake up and to see that he isn't you. The second step is to awaken for the purpose of finding out where this thief is so that he can be watched. Then the third step is that when he is located, keeping an eye on him to see what he's doing, his patterns, what he's wearing, his style, mannerisms, looks, etc. Eventually, there is so much pressure on this thief that the lights come on and he flees the house. Better yet, realizing that he isn't you and is just a figment of imagination, puts an instant end to him right then and there, sort of realizing your shadow isn't you.

Do you get this on a feeling, seeing, intellectual, intuitive, and experiential level? For the latter experiential understanding, just see the reactions in the ego right now to all of this, if it's agreeing with this, whatever it wants to say to reply to this, any opinions ideas it has about this is all the reactions of the ego, and its being seen in direct experience right now.

Adam: Yeah this is all so wild and I definitely see it. Almost feel the need to not want to reply because then I know it's the thief that replied.

Dom: Don't worry too much about responding as the thief, when Union manifests, you can reply, move, act, communicate from the place of Union and it will be the most sincere and genuine way of communicating.

I'll give you another example; you've watched movies before on a flat screen TV right?

Adam: Yup

Dom: So tell me what happens when you watch a movie, what is it like, thoughts, feeling, emotions, perception, etc. You don't even have to answer right away, but take it as some homework. Maybe watch a movie with your girl next few days and report back what you find while still allowing the continuous process of seeing the ego, not identifying, making it habitual, and feeling things out in the meantime.

Adam: So we watched a movie, Life of Pi, and I was so wrapped up in it, I really wasn't even aware of myself or my girl. I mean, there were quite a few times where I reminded myself like, "Hey this is supposed to be homework, so make sure you pay attention to all the things that are happening." But they were few and far between, but when I did pause to recollect and watch, it's like I snapped out of being lost in the movie and came back to my senses and the rest of the things going on around me. But when lost in the movie, there were just emotions of all sorts and reactions to what I was seeing.

Dom: Okay good, really good insights. Were you aware that you were watching a movie on a screen, and that the screen was limited in size compared to the rest of the surroundings in the room?

Adam: Lol, I just face palmed for not catching that bro, that's crazy but you're right when I look back on movie night. I just entirely missed that one.

Dom: And what about the movie itself, did you ever consider or speculate that the main character is just acting, just pretending for the cameras, and the tiger is trained and probably harmless enough to be able to act with the main character along with the other animals? And did you notice that the plot is made up, and all the different symbology, camera angles, lighting, etc?

Adam: Nope, missed that too. I was mostly paying attention to how I would lose myself in the movie and when I stepped back for a bit, I became aware of more details but the movie lost its reality until I gave it my full attention.

Dom: So this is the same thing with the Ego, it is just a fake imagined actor with its own imagined characteristics, plots, motives, ideas, likes/dislikes, opinions, philosophies, sins, hardships, past, and so forth.

And the screen that the illusion based actor plays its roles on, is in the front of the head, wrapping itself around the watcher of the movie, making the watcher entranced by his act so that the watcher completely loses himself into the illusion of the ego movie.

So back to your comment here: "but when I did pause to recollect and watch, it's like I snapped out of being lost in the movie and came back to my senses and the rest of the things going on around me." Remember that? Now this same thing has to apply to all the live and active day dream movie illusions the ego produces, so there is a continuous return to one's senses, and a seeing that this is all just a fake movie playing out.

And back to this comment here: "But when lost in the movie, there were just emotions of all sorts and reacts to what I was seeing." The same thing will happen when you lose yourself in the ego daydreams.

And back to my comment here: "Were you aware that you were watching a movie on a screen, and that the screen was limited in size compared to the rest of the surroundings in the room?" Now apply that to the Ego and see that when it does arise with its illusions, there is also a body going on, and seeing is happening, and hearing is happening, and perceiving is happening, and there is a present moment experience of all of this which is very simple and peaceful. Doing this will loosen the lies and illusions of the fake movie of ego.

And last is this comment here just to reiterate: "And what about the movie itself, did you ever consider or speculate that the main character is just acting, just pretending for the cameras, etc" Means to see how the ego acts one way around the girlfriend, another way around teachers, yet another way around strangers, then another way around the homeless, then a different way around an attractive woman, and how it might lie or produce white lies, or be dishonest, hide things, be scared of other things, have biases of various sorts, maybe even think it's better than others, and so on.

This is examining and seeing all the details of the ego and allowing all these things to come to surface in different scenarios and experiences so they can be seen, no longer identified with, and no longer played out unconsciously in real life.

Doing all those things above is part of this continuous process that will pull off the mask that is the ego so that it is seen as just an imagined illusion with no inherent reality of its own, the grand cosmic joke to laugh at, with a sigh of relief when there is a realization that this heavy identity doesn't have to be carried around anymore, like a heavy anvil being dropped so a lightness of life occurs. So spend a few days or the rest of the week with this and tell me what you find, understood?

Adam: Yeah I got it. This really groundbreaking stuff, I honestly don't understand why this isn't being taught at schools and in the Church, something so fundamental and important, and yet if we don't see the ego, we miss it entirely by getting wrapped up in its movie just like your description. Even me saying all of this, that's all part of the movie of that same ego, only this time I'm aware of the words being formed just before I type them, or like you say, this is all happening on its own. I will take some time like you said and sit with this new perspective over the next few days and get back to you and just wanted to show some gratitude and appreciation for your work with me by stating a deep and heartfelt thank you.

Note * It was about a week later I heard back from Adam again, and while the insights did begin to pour into him, the lack of structure and discipline kept him fully submersed in the ego's day dream movie screen.

Adam: Hey Dom, just checking back in after a busy week with work, school and all the other life stuff and wanted to report back after applying all of this over the past week and I'm just completely wrapped up in the day dream and it really sucks. Yeah sure there were times throughout the day of sort of pulling back and watching what the ego is doing, but then you know, you get busy with the next thing, schedules, work, assignments, girlfriend, it's all so much throughout the day and I'm just completely wrapped up all sorts of identities, and to be honest I'm salty about this whole thing and not being able to catch it in time.

So the times I do catch the movie, I sort of have this pause where I step back and watch what's happening with the ego but also all around me, like when I watched the movie with my girl and was more conscious of the other things going on besides the movie. Sure it works in that moment, but that moment doesn't last long at all because say I get a text message or facebook notification, which pulls me right back into the screen of the ego movie, and it's not until hours later that I'll stop again to have another step back, and that's on a good day if I'm lucky.

So that got me to thinking, you said you do week long retreats with people and I'm thinking about just making it up that way by you during my next school break to really work on this with more focus and discipline without all the life distractions, or in the very least, set aside more time to really sit with this to be able to step back from that ego movie a lot more. Can you tell me next time you're holding a retreat or at least give me some tips on how to structure my day?

Dom: Okay, so first before we get to structures and retreats and all of that, if you could just see that this 'I' is just a thought, and examine whether this thought is any different than the thought of a flying pink elephant, or a black unicorn, or a gnome. Seriously check and see if there's any difference.

Look at that whole reply above and look how many 'I's' there are in the statement. There is nothing that needs to change in life. For example, I'm not asking you to stop going to school, or take less classes, or spend less time at work, with friends, with your girlfriend and so forth. The point is to allow all these things to continue to happen, but to see that they are all happening all on their own, without a 'you' who is doing them.

The whole "movie' example we discussed previously, this day dream movie the ego is constantly playing out, it does so all day long from the moment the body wakes up, until the last moment before sleep, that ego movie is always there playing out all of its stories about the past, present, future all revolving around this thought 'I' and it continues to do so all day long. So while my example was specifically designed to give you insight into the ego and what it does, to say that "I want to figure out how to stop this ego and detach from its daydream" is a trap because that is creating another 'I' that wants to get rid of the 'I', do you see this?

Or with the whole retreat scenario as well, do you see how the ego has created this story that, "If 'I' go do this retreat with Dom with less distractions, then 'I' will be able to detach from this daydream ego movie?" This is the creation of an illusion daydream based future scenario and imagining, via daydreams, that at some later time in the future, this whole thing will be resolved, when in reality there is only the present moment, that identity and illusion that believes it will get something at some time in the future, isn't even anything real other than the belief in an imagined Santa Claus based nonexistent character. If this could be seen to be so, right at this very moment, then everything could be resolved at this very point in time. Seeing all of this for longer and clearer periods of time will resolve the unreality of the ego.

Another thing is in the beauty of your current lifestyle, where there are all these mini micro retreats going on all day long if you can start to see how each moment is its own separate micro event, which eventually flows into the next event.

So for example, when the body wakes up in the morning, whether to an alarm or sleeping in on a day off, that moment of the body awakening, is a micro event of that exact action happening, and that micro event has its own style of identity going on in the daydream of the ego.

That imagined identity usually looks like this, "Aww man, it's so early, wish I can sleep in today. I'll go back to sleep until the alarm goes off again in five minutes, then have to brush my teeth, pee/urinate, for breakfast I think

I'll make some scrambled eggs if there is time, and if not then a bagel with some cream cheese, or maybe with butter and jam depending on how I feel by then. I can't believe that movie I watched last night, it was crazy with an insane plot, and even my girlfriend liked it as well, I wish she would have stayed the night instead of going back to her dorm room," and so on and so forth, all revolving around this 'I'.

So let's look at this objectively at what's going on. There is a body lying there which was just awakened by an alarm in a room and there seem to be a bunch of imagined thoughts appearing about a vast array of topics centering around this imagined 'I'.

Is this micro event all one thing? The room, the body, all the senses, the sound of the alarm, the day dreams, the space in the room, are they all one event, one thing? This is how we play with restructuring perspective so as to pop this bias bubble of illusion, by reexamining reality. Are there any divisions and separation of all the elements in that micro event, or are divisions/separations only imagined to be so by the daydream ego movie screen?

So then what happens? Eventually the next micro event is, the actual physical body getting out of the bed, walking over to the bathroom, and all the habitual actions that happen in that bathroom which usually consist of brushing teeth, urination/excretion, and possibly a quick shower.

So now in this next micro event, that Egoic daydream movie screen is imagining the next set of illusions, and the imagined identity usually looks something like this, "Ahhh minty fresh toothpaste, feels good. Now I just have to pee and then jump into the shower real quick. Oh crap, I forget to bring in my clothes that I'm going to wear for today. That's okay, I'll just shower real quick and then dress after the shower. Yeah, I think I'll do the bagel with cream cheese with some orange juice instead of the butter and jam. Sure wish my girl would have stayed over last night. I wonder what she meant by that post on facebook about wanting to visit Europe in the summer. I forgot to ask her about that last night because of the movie, but I'll ask her later today when I see her. Let me just check my texts and facebook real quick on my phone before jumping in the shower.

So again, looking at the scene objectively, yes, all those things are happening physically, and yes, all those imagined scenarios and conceptualized daydreams are also playing out, but all of this is happening on its own, and not to anyone. The whole micro event is one whole thing. The body, the toothbrush, the toilet, the water pouring out of the shower, the bathroom itself, the space in it, it's all One thing and any divisions and separations are only occurring as imagined illusions in the mind.

So after this, the next micro event begins, along with the imagined identity creating a whole new set of daydreamed illusions around the next set of circumstances.

So this is the beauty of processing all of these teachings within the realms of regular life, with all of its different micro events, allows there to be a seeing how the Egoic daydream movie screen changes its labels, divisions, separations, opinions, ideas, concepts around all the different scenarios.

Now sure, you can still come to a retreat, however not with any illusion or daydreamed constructs such as follows, "as long as 'I' get there, then 'I' will get resolution." It has to be approached in the right inbetweenness, from a place of no assumptions, openness, flow, and other factors that I have outlined in a list for retreat goers, and yes, in the retreats people do have huge breakthroughs to various degrees, and sometimes into Union. However, once they return to the regular schedules of life and enter into all of those micro events that bring out different imagined and emotional illusion based aspects of the ego daydream movie, then it can be easy to wrap back up into a belief of that illusion, and lose the access to Union.

So with you, you're tackling the entire thing in regular usual life, and if there is some deep inner intuitive draw to go into solitude or spend time in retreat to integrate and stabilize Union, then it can be done so at a later date and coming from that angle, do you see what I'm saying?

Adam: Yeah I See what you're saying, and right now there is this feeling of not having any need to even say anything anymore or to ask any more questions. It's like a feeling of being done with everything, but also a feeling like that no matter what angle I try to approach this from in terms of saying anything, that's already ego, even this whole comment.

Dom: Yeah, that's definitely a good insight except it can cause a lot of imbalance. We need to communicate with others in life, work, relationships, and it's part of life. So it's also not about no longer saying anything, it's more so the ability to communicate but at the same time, seeing that communication is happening, all on its own, without any communicator. And seeing the way the words are framed just before being spoken, or as they are spoken, or when someone else is speaking, seeing and watching that this listening and understanding of words is happening, all on its own, and no one is there who is doing this, like the micro events mentioned above.

Adam: Yeah, I get completely what you're saying, Ha it even feels strange to say this 'I' because I'm starting to, scratch that, there is a seeing of this 'I' now and what it does. I see too how there are all these traps, subtle ways that it wraps itself around events and actions like in the micro events. It's funny because when I read your emails or we go into chat, just pointing this out makes me crazy super aware of everything that's happening, and it's very easy to get into this feeling that it's all happening on its own, but then when this exchange ends and there is an entry into the next micro events that make up the day, there is a loss of this super awareness.

So I want to ask about how to structure my day around all of this, but I see now if I say that I want to create this super awareness of all things to be there, then it creates this subtle 'I' identification around wanting to keep this heightened sense going. So that's one of those traps right?

Dom: Yeah exactly, that's another trap. This heightened sense of awareness of all things going on will grow on its own and help to show and shine light on what the ego is doing, and also shine light on whether or not the ego is anything real, or just a constant TV screen featuring a movie about an imagined 'I', or not. As long as all these angles are played with and reexamined throughout the day, it'll start building steam, and if not, then there is a return of illusion and Egoic life.

So if you wanted a blueprint to Union and how a schedule looks regarding applying these blueprints in your daily life, here's how something like that would look like:

Set the alarm for 20 minutes early than what time you usually wake up, and on days off if there is the ability to sleep in, then staying in bed for an extra

20 minutes without falling back asleep. Then spending that 20 minutes just watching and seeing what the ego is doing, watching the ego's dialogue, thoughts, opinions, plans, illusions, how it references that thought 'I' around all the aforementioned aspects.

Now added to this, should be the seeing that this ego process isn't who you are, it is just something that is happening on its own. Seeing this and feeling that this Egoic imagined movie isn't who you are.

Now added to this should be the seeing/realizing that besides the imagined movie daydream ticker tape, constantly pumping out 'I' centered Santa clause based daydreams, there are other things going on besides what's playing on the screen. There are also the senses, hearing, seeing, breathing, that morning breath taste in the mouth, the whole body laying there and having this seeing/realizing that all of this is also happening, all on its own, along with the ego imagined daydreams happening all on their own.

Don't worry, it seems like a lot, but it's very simple and easy the more this is done, like learning to ride a bike. Still with me? Okay, going on further.

So as all the other aspects that are going on are noticed (senses, breathing, body, etc), all these things are also seen as not who you are. So there should be this attentiveness of the eyes seeing with the intellectual understanding that: The eyes are seeing but there is no seer. The eyes are seeing all on their own. Now also add to that the feeling that these eyes aren't you, they are their own existence/sense that is happening all on its own. So there is the attentiveness of the eyes/seeing, then the intellectual reminder that this process is happening all on its own, then getting a feeling for what this is like that these eyes/seeing isn't you and that eyes/seeing are/is happening all on its own without an 'I' necessary.

Now do the same for the other senses, the breath, then eventually the whole body, then last before finally getting up from bed, applying the same to the ego, i.e. the ego/imagination/daydream/illusions are occurring, but I am not the ego. Then the reminder that this ego is happening all on its own and there is no "ego'er" who is doing the "egoing". Then getting a feel for this like what was done with the eyes/seeing, and the rest of the senses.

If it seems complicated now, save this in your tablet, cell phone, or a paper printout to have quick access to around the bed, because this same thing will be repeated at night, because the schedule includes going to sleep 20 minutes early specifically for this practice, except with one caveat. When applying this at night, there should be an added addition of seeing that falling asleep is starting to occur without a sleeper, all on its own, so this sense, understanding, feeling is established as the last thing before deep sleep and the first thing in the morning as the body wakes up.

So with the above first thing in the morning practice and last thing at night practice established, now we can start to involve the rest of the day. That the same practice as mentioned above, can be applied throughout the day during lunch breaks, driving/travel, down time, bathroom breaks, and squeezed in wherever possible.

Remember the micro events? This is the application of this same practice as above to the micro events. So, for example, when doing the morning practice, the next micro event would be to physically get out of bed and enter into the whole bathroom event. So this whole seeing/feeling process can continue to be carried (without anyone carrying it) into the next event. So instead of, "Okay, I did the morning practice and have to get up now to start the day," that thought process should be seen before it even has the chance to arise in the ego movie screen that you are now aware of, then instantly dropping/surrendering that imagined frame of thought, and instead, seeing and feeling that the morning practice has come to an end all on its own, and physically getting up off the bed to start the day is happening all on its own, and it's happening to no one.

The walking to the bathroom is happening all on its own with no walker who is doing it. The brushing of teeth in front of the mirror is happening all on its own, and the imagined ego based daydream of imaginations about the rest of that day, is also happening all on its own and there is no "ego'er" who is doing the "egoing."

Eventually this same feeling and seeing sense of everything being impersonal will be established into more and more micro events of the day, and this will happen all on its own in the form of grace, because what will start to happen is that losing yourself in the imagined illusion character of 'I', in whatever micro event is occurring will feel completely unnatural and alien to you, and when the false illusion of the 'I' is brought to attention, it can be surrendered and let go as something that is just a Santa clause based illusion, that it is something which isn't you, and that everything is happening all on its own in the micro event, without a "you" anywhere in it. That ego is literally not real, just like a daydream is not real.

As long as this process continues in this way, it will pick up the steam and kinetic energy that I speak of in other exchanges, and will lead to huge insights which grace brings to attention. So for example there can be a micro event like being around friends, and someone says something stupid or inappropriate, which causes annoyance/irritability to arise in you and to speak out against this person about what was said.

Now a regular person would never be aware of what is happening within them, and will unconsciously react to what was said. But for you, there will be a seeing of the irritability arising, a seeing of the ego wrapping its identity around this emotion and having this need to react based on the motivation of the irritability. In any moment of this process, there can be a pause, and a dropping/letting go and no longer identifying with either of these processes. Of course, when you're starting out with this, in the beginning you won't see or catch any of this, or if you do, it will be moments later, but that's okay, the process is like wine and needs time to ripen

Additionally, with all of the above I just mentioned, on how each day should look like, this is just a small portion of the blueprints and a basic approximation of how the retreats I hold are also formulated. There is much more to this. As this process continues, various insights arise, grace, the ego eventually starts to become unglued and that requires another set of blueprints to handle. Do you understand Adam?

Adam: Yeah understood, just reading the blueprints basically blew my mind wide open, just the scope of it all is really massive and similarly I'm just watching the reactions of the ego play out, and some pretty deep insights happening already.

So one of the insights that came up is when I reconstruct everything that happened in my life just yesterday. First off, I'm not even aware of and can't remember every single micro event of the day, but the more I reflect, the more returns to memory. So just analyzing yesterday's micro events, I notice that the ego has a different set of illusions that arise around different micro events. So the Egoic elements of the day dream are different at home than they are at work, or when spending time with the girlfriend, or in class, or when other attractive girls pass me on campus, or different when at church, or when replying to you. It's all just a really massive view to have, like a very large contextual palate of life I guess if I was to put it that way, and then it's so funny because in the grand scheme of things there seems to be this feeling that "hey, maybe there really isn't a me, maybe like Dom is saying, this supposed "me" is in the way of this grand scheme, ha!" Or perhaps like he said, there is no 'me' in the first place because it's imagined.

I'm also interested in this next set of blueprints with the insights and ego ungluing but I see how the 'I' is wrapping around this identity of "oh, more blueprints! I must have! I must get!" So that's the ego daydream within the context of this specific micro event that's happening right now, and I'm able to see it, and let it go.

Dom: Yeah that's it, see! Pretty easy, but it just has to keep going, keep gaining steam through every micro event and X amount of time spent in this way.

Adam: Yeah that makes it much easier, that explanation and just watching the fingers type on the keyboard, and the ego provides the words to type, and the watching of reading your replies, oh and the realization of all the ego games on facebook, that one's probably the most difficult to deal with because when I examine my own identity, so much of it relies on everything I do on there. Do you recommend maybe easing off of it a bit?

Dom: That whole insight about facebook is part of grace showing you how everything is structured to perpetuate the ego, and the question about easing off of Facebook is an intuitive insight on how to handle that, and yes of course I highly recommend easing off of facebook, especially during this ongoing process. When you do use it, see it as a micro event, and see how the ego wraps itself around 'I', how it wants to respond to all the different posts, opinions, and games played by all the other egos that are on there.

There is a ton of Egoic psychological fragmentation that happens on facebook. First off, people mostly post only the good things about themselves and their lives. So right off the bat, you're seeing a false illusion that each person constructs on how they want everyone else to see them.

You rarely see people discuss marital issues, depressions, addictions, existential crises, and so forth, and these are things everyone deals with. Second, there is a "grass is greener on the other side illusion" going on as well. People post pictures or videos of vacations, or a new house, new car, or a new pet, and your ego then says, "they look happy with that, so if 'I' have that, then 'I' will be happy as well." That illusion is a lie because then it sets off a chain of reactions, such as "I have to do whatever it takes to also go on vacation, and I won't be happy until I finally get a new car just like the other guy." And these things cause issues, emotional hurts, and additional imagined Egoic identity which further blocks Union with God.

Adam: Yeah that's crazy as well, it's like that whole context you gave me about all of the micro events and how each one has its own set of Egoic identifications and elements, the whole facebook world is like a whole other set of this same thing, like all the micro events that are online are also each causing ego identifications and illusions, wow that's insane. Everyone will think I'm crazy for getting off there though.

Dom: Being worried about what others will think is another Egoic identity based on a reaction and emotion. This has to be seen when it arises, deconstructed, seen as not you, and surrendered. Can you do that now?

Adam: Yeah, going through it now. It's not as easy as the other stuff so it seems. There's this big investment in the self identity based on the approval of others and all the groups of people and circles I'm part of. That worry about the thoughts of others is pretty big.

Dom: Take your time with this Adam, the bigger things take some time to process and disidentify from, but it's vital to go through it. Also, only what God thinks of you matters, and not what anyone else thinks, and God is waiting to be experienced when all of these worries and identifications are detached from and surrendered. He's already there, all around you, in you, everywhere always and the experience of this will dawn if the grace continues to flourish. As for the facebook account, you don't have to delete it, I have one as well. Just see that there is a balance around its use. If you use it to send a message to someone, for work, relationships, contacts, planning, and so on then use it. But spending hours on there and getting wrapped up in the micro event ego games is a complete and utter waste of time when that time is better spent in meditation, going for a walk, applying these teachings to a variety of experiences like talking to others (talking is happening without a talker), getting some exercise (without an exerciser), and so on.

Adam: Yeah, I get the point and at this point there's almost this deep inner want and need to simplify all the things that cause all the crazy ego traps. This all feels very therapeutic as well, like a lifting of all the heavy anvils of various social identities for the sake of being very simple and present.

I have to get going, but I'm already applying all of this as we speak. Thanks so much again for all of these teachings, feels like I can't give thanks enough Dom!

Dom: All thanks to God, in his Oneness and Omnipresence. Just shoot me back an e-mail if anything new pops up, questions, hang ups, clarifications and so forth.

Note* A week later, Adam writes back.

Adam: Hey Dom what's going on. So I just wanted to give you an update on the past week and had a question about something that happened last night that I don't quite understand. In the past week, I really got the hang of seeing all the micro events and how the ego displays different patterns in each one and there is much more peace and stillness it seems. But the biggest thing for me personally is doing the night time practice just like you described. I've been having some really crazy dreams lately, but last night was the craziest of all. I literally woke up about 4 a.m. and was seeing the ego completely detached, and I got scared and didn't know what to do. It was doing all these strange things like bringing up past memories and showing all these various visions and insights and just really wild stuff, only it wasn't me at all doing any of this. It was like you say, doing what the ego does all on its own, but I completely freaked out and got scared. Haven't slept since and was wondering what that was and what do I do next.

Dom: Yeah that's just the ego becoming unglued, and the fear of that happening is also the ego attaching itself to fear and confusion so as to perpetuate its glue and identity. This is all part of the process and next time it happens, just relax, be surrendered, loose, breath calmly, and continue this process of no longer identifying with anything the ego does, shows, or any emotions, fears, confusions that arise, and that 'I', all the while continuing with the set of instructions and blueprints as I've already sent. This ungluing will happen more and more until the whole ego structure finally comes off and falls away.

Also notice how nothing else really changed. There is still a body, senses, breathing, sleeping, awakening, life and everything in it still goes on, however it goes on with an unglued ego, so don't get caught up in freaking out or getting over excited about these experiences starting to manifest. Just being present with that micro event of the "ungluing of the ego" and seeing all the reactions of the ego, of its own ungluing, and not identifying with any of that. Give it another week or so and continue to gain the steam and grace of this process.

Adam: Got it! I will get back to you with an update next week. Thanks again.

Less than a few days later, Adam wrote back.

Adam: Hey Dom, okay so it happened again, but this time things seem to be permanent, or at least semi-permanent. So the ungluing thing happened again, and this time I sat with it without freaking out like you said. Same thing as last time, got awakened in the middle of the night and there it was, completely unhinged, and the watching of what it was doing was occurring, just being still and continued to stay calm and breath, and of course a ton of fear mixed with exhilaration.

So as I was just being with this, there was this definite detachment and ungluing completely from the ego, like this huge distance now between seeing it, and the ego illusions themselves all acting wildly like some crazy spoiled child that's angry and craving attention. Lots of stuff came up, fears, resistance, lots of interesting ideas about the future, various insights, it was just so much coming up and it was really difficult to be with this without getting caught up in the whole thing.

Eventually, while just surrendering to the whole process, sleep happened again, and when the alarm went off, I woke up but there was no ego there. I didn't know who I was, where I was, what was what, where was what, and yet everything was still the same like you mentioned, breathing and seeing were still going on, life was still happening at that point but there weren't any filters or any angles to anything. It was just pure and fresh, hard to describe.

So then as I'm up, sitting in bed after having turned the alarm off, I watch as the ego finally makes its delayed appearance into the head area so it can start its day dream. It's so crazy! It's like the ego was late to start the day, and it was entirely non-existent for those few minutes, then finally when it did arrive, there was still this vast distance from it and it's not like it used to be. It's almost like it can't glue itself back into an Egoic identity like it used to be.

So now after a couple of days, it's like the ego is completely unglued most of the day, and it has nowhere to stick, kind of like a nonstick frying pan, and the only time it still does have some stickiness to it is when I get a facebook notifications or someone asks me something out of the blue and catches me off guard, then there's like this momentary identity, but soon as it's seen, it falls away again, it's so obvious that this thing, these illusions aren't me. They are more like imagined reference points, but really it seems like reality itself doesn't have any reference points, it's pure. Also, when people call me by my name, it's like I have to remind myself that the label, the name Adam, is my own reference point and that maybe I should respond, it's pretty funny actually and I laughed a bit about that. So that's what's going on now, just wondering if this is good progress and wondering if you can tell me about that period where there was no ego and absolutely zero reference points.

Dom: Yeah sure, the progress is good and you're in this period and stage of the "no-stick mind" as you called it with the clever nonstick frying pan example. So this is the ego's inability to be able to glue itself to you as a false identity, but there is still some "glue" that remains in those unexpected situations and that also has to be caught and seen through, and this will become automatic eventually. The name as a label and needing a reminder to respond is another good sign. You're right, the name Adam is just a label that is imagined, and it also is not who you are.

As for the pure unknowingness and zero reference points, that's a good sign, that Pure Unknowingness is just an in between stage that can be used to purify the rest of all the Egoic illusion activity and the identification with the body. Some people pass through this stage quickly, others seem to marinate here for a bit longer as a means or platform for a thorough purification of all the arising illusions and constructs. Next time that happens, if you can remember to, or at least intuit, just let that unknowingness be there and surrender into it deeply, a full surrender and letting go downwards, deeper into the body, like falling into the heart by surrendering to gravity.

The next stage is for the Seer/Seeing, which is now free and unglued from the ego, to vertically fall down into Union. It feels like falling from the head area, down into something very deep and unknown, which ends up being Union, and this is where surrender, letting go, looseness, relaxation comes in.

Do you understand this as the next step? I sent you an exchange to read where I mention having this deep physical letting go and surrender along the rest of the practices, so read that and make sure to comprehend and apply to your own practice.

Adam: Yeah, I remember you sent me an exchange with Michael and mentioned it to him there, I'll read this one you sent as well, and I think I'm starting to feel what you're talking about. When there is a deep physical surrender of the body, things just seem to open up more, like more peace, and just being okay with everything and I'm so used to surrendering into the sleep practice during the night, so I'll spend some time with this and get back to you.

Note* At this point I didn't hear from Adam for about three weeks and it was vital to stay in touch, but I knew things can go one of two ways, either he would get wrapped back up in some aspect(s) of ego identification and the life scenarios that make that happen, or he would fully see this through since he had already uncovered a milestone of a signpost in the ungluing of the ego. So I sent him a message to check up on him.

Dom: Hey Adam, just a courtesy check to see how things are unraveling in the process.

Adam: Hey Dom I was just thinking about sending you a quick shout to give you an update, then I opened up the laptop and there was your e-mail, pretty cool!

As far as the ego, yeah this thing is completely unglued, it's all a nonstick frying pan, it has nowhere to stick at all and no matter what it tries to do with any fears or excitement or reactions, it's pretty much instantaneously seen through and impossible to get wrapped up in any of it anymore. Also with the surrender, you were right, I had a huge moment where there was this deep falling into Oneness, it was crazy, everything was One thing and I disappeared into it and of course I wanted to jump up and celebrate the entrance into Union, but then it all disappeared, like instead of the dropping down, there was a rising back up into the head area and right back into this in between stage of being unglued from the ego, but not yet Union.

It's tricky, because ever since then, I've been trying to wrap my head around it and get back there, but then I remember reading in some of the exchanges how wanting to get back there is another Egoic identity, so yeah I saw that and just let that go. I figured that since it was this deep and wholesome letting go like you mention that caused this drop into Union, then only surrender will make that happen. Only now it's like I see that there can be an attachment of identification with the need to surrender to get back to Union. The thing is, since all of that is seen, it can't stick, so I just allow this surrender to take place all on its own mostly at night, but there hasn't been any Union experience since then.

Dom: Yeah it's very subtle. Just make sure there is a loving and wholesome surrender and letting go of the body, and almost like the "seeing" process, that whole structure that sees the ego which has nowhere to stick; now there has to be an unsticking of the 'Seeing' so that the seer drops back into Union, a disidentification from the Seeing.

Most likely there is a subtle identification with the watching/seeing process and that's what is holding up Union. See that's a bit trickier, so you have to go back into the night time practice just before sleep and do as follows. When you are scanning the body and seeing it as a body happening without a bodier, seeing each of the senses as happening without a hearer, seer, breather, bodier, sleeper, etc, now the same thing should be applied to the "Awareness/Seeing" process.

That awareness which is aware of all of these things not being you, also has to have this impersonal disidentification applied to it as well. So awareness is aware of all these other things, but there is no aware'er. That awareness is happening on its own but it isn't who you are. So there should be this surrendering and letting go of awareness itself as well, along with the rest of the aspects of the body, senses, thoughts, emotions, etc, like you have been doing.

There is just an imbalance in this awareness as it probably has felt, up to this point, like this is who you are since the ego has become unglued and won't stick anywhere. So give this a go for a few days or a week, because some people get stuck at this portion of a very subtle identification with awareness, and that has to also be deconstructed and surrendered.

It's basically just awareness resting in itself, gently aware of itself and resting in itself in downward surrender with no expectations, no identities, nowhere to hold on to.

Adam: Yeah, that sounds about right. Interestingly enough, when I apply the night time practice, I haven't been applying the teachings to the seer at all, guess I forgot about that part. So this actually makes sense. Okay I'll write back in a few.

Note* Again, this time around it took Adam about a week to deconstruct the identity with awareness so that it would lead into a very deep and long Union experience.

Adam: It happened bro! I broke through into it, like you said with the awareness deal, it finally happen and it was so long probably like a few hours of Union. The next day it started sneaking up on me, I was walking to class but there wasn't any me anywhere to be found, just incredibly fascinating and my girlfriend has noticed the last few months all the changes that have occurred and I think it's rubbing off on her. I gave her some of your e-mails and she's been checking them out, this is all so crazy, I would have never in a million years believed any of this was possible, just absolutely overjoyed at this point, with really no one there to be overjoyed, craziest paradox ever! It's all legit, 100% real just like you've been saying, it's almost like being freed from some matrix we're all living in. This is just beyond the scope of everything I ever thought, I mean I can't even really tell anyone anything about this because they would have to see for themselves to really get it!

So yeah, the Union sneaks up on me, kind of comes and goes on its own accord and there's really nothing I can do to make it happen or not happen. So just being in this very loose sense of self, or rather loose sense of everything seems to be the trick. But when I talk to others it goes away, so of course the question is if this will ever become permanent like you mentioned in some of the other exchanges? Wow! I'm just speechless.

Dom: Yeah, congrats! This is just the beginning, and now from here on out this Union has to be integrated and stabilized so it's always there within each micro event of each day. So now there will be a noticing of the things that allow Union to be there or not be there, and a sort of clearing the last remnants of the things that keep Union from being there at all times, by using the experiences in the micro events to learn from them as to the nuances and subtleties of what keeps Union at bay.

So when talking to others, there has to be a studying and noticing where there might be any physical tension, Egoic identification, if awareness is entirely wrapped up in the external micro event of the conversation, and if it is, having this loose surrender and step back from the conversation so there is this room to concurrently drop vertically back into the Oneness while still holding the conversation. It's learning to balance, like walking on a razor's edge or a tightrope. Give this time, this is just the beginning and there's much more on the way.

Adam: Yeah, that makes complete sense. I was already starting to feel that this was the case and you just locked it all down for me. I really want to thank you for this, it really means a lot. Let me know if you need help with your videos or a website or anything, and I'll make sure to give back. Truly incredible how that Oneness is there all along right in front of us, but we don't see because of the blindness of ego stuff or identifying with all these different things. So this is the part where Christ says the He and the Father are One? This is just the most incredible, I can't even really finish this sentence, everything is beyond words, ha!

Dom: Yeah, that's the same Oneness. All thanks and gratitude to the One, and I'll let you know when I could use some of your tech support for sure. Also, just check back in every so often if anything pops up along the way.

It's good to hear from the people that finally uncover Union that it's still there years after the initial access and if your girlfriend is interested in going to distance, tell her to contact me and I'll send her all the exchanges so she can figure this all out as well.

Adam: Yeah for sure, I already told her to send you an e-mail, but there's a lot of resistance and she's asking a ton of questions the last few weeks. She's like how I was when I first contacted you, haha! Alright brother, I'll be in touch. One love, One God, One life, One Christ!

***

A subtle picture of a person having ego

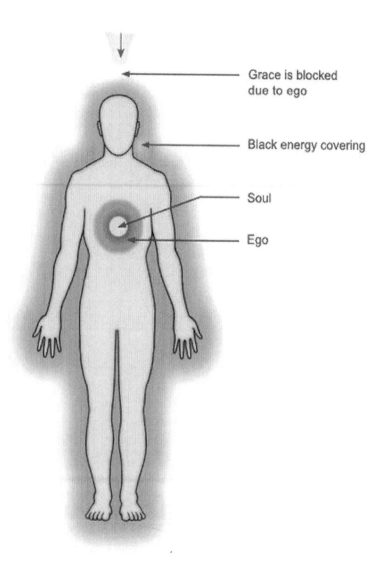

Grace is blocked due to ego

Black energy covering

Soul

Ego

CHAPTER 3

HAYLEY'S EXCHANGE

As with most people, Hayley came across the YouTube videos and there was an intuitive connection that arose in her from watching the videos. This is usually how I know that deeper teachings can be shared with people from Christian backgrounds without the need for debates or theological discussions, when there is that intuitive connection in the first place. To this day, it is something that I continue to deeply feel from her even though there is a vast distance and ocean separating us. To those who have accessed even a single glimpse of Union, there is a deeper unspeakable acknowledgement and simple Love.

Hayley, a hair stylist from Bristol, U.K., contacted me during a very trying and extremely busy period of my life, the details of which are unnecessary, but the context of which is important to note. There was still very much a scattering of philosophies, as in my own experience, I had come to period of realizing there is so much more to Union than I could have ever imagined, and my notes/writings were an unorganized mess. So the majority of people I was working with were locals over the phone, in person, and only about once or twice a month if that.

Even though my initial exchange with her wasn't as laser focused as it could have been, given the circumstances, I learned some important lessons of my own when loosely working with her; that you never know who will break through and when. This is all very unpredictable, but the feeling, the intuitive sense, and the examples for other people to comprehend and practically apply to themselves, can really open the doors to Grace and Union.

Hayley: Hello, I got your email address from your YouTube posts, I hope you don't mind me contacting you personally, they are years old?

I just wanted to thank you for your wonderful teachings on youtube. I have listened to your posts, and they have touched my heart beyond belief. You have a wealth of knowledge. I feel impelled to seek Him deeper and more consciously than ever before with your encouragement. I am a girl who doesn't belong to a church, but have been brought up with the Christian faith, but have not officially attended a church for 7-10 years. So I have recently, the past 18 months seemed to rekindle my love for God all alone. But this by no means makes my belief any weaker or insignificant. Anyways I won't ramble on too much now! Thank you for your ace videos on youtube, you are an inspiration, please keep them coming

Dom: Hey Hayley, no don't mind the e-mail. It brings joy to the heart to know that you understand the video on the level of soul.

Not sure if you have access to Union with the Father yet or not, but there is a number of ways to access this, either through the subconscious, or through awareness/surrender of Egoic/body identity. If I knew where you were at in your mystical growth, I can give you more advice/guidance. In the meantime however, I will send you some material to check out that will deepen your access to Union/God within.

Note* At this point I had a three or four books, written by other authors that I was passing out and really loosely basing my work with people on besides my own Union, however several of these, even though they perfectly describe what the ego does, what it is, how it operates, and so forth, were still eventually giving exercises and practices that "you" needed to do. So instead of seeing that, who you think you are is an illusion, daydream, false identity that can be seen through on the spot, some of these other books were then saying you still need cultivate a practice that you are doing, instead of cultivating the seeing that the 'I' is just a thought. So I sent these preliminary books in the midst of my own busy period and for the sake of giving her some deeper context of what the ego is and does. Each of these books had its strengths and weaknesses and there was this ongoing intuitive sense on how to remove all the weaknesses, while keeping all the strengths in order to distill and purify something more potent.

Hayley: Good morning Dom

I've just woken up to your email thanks for replying! I'm not really sure but I think I'm kind of at the very beginning of this journey, tuning in. This whole experience feels very personal.
Physically I feel His/Their presence constantly, I am feeling very "light and fluffy", and a lot of love.

He is on my mind and in my thoughts constantly. I pray a lot, and am trying to meditate and be still and empty my mind, (which I find tricky sometimes).

Thanks for the literature, will get stuck in to those ASAP.

Dom: Of course, the relationship, eventual Union, with God is always super personal.
All those feelings are great, the lightness, love, constant presence......so the rest is really surrender, letting go, meditation, seeing through and giving up the ego/I, and to become completely unraveled if you will, which will reveal the deepest unified access to
God.

If you dive into those materials it will all makes sense. In the meantime, if any questions arise, feel free to give me a shout.

Hayley: Hey Dom

First, I just wanted to thank you for the books you gave me, they are fab, (although it's taking me ages to get through the first x3!) However, for the first time it's all becoming crystal clear.
I'm starting to peel back the layers to reveal myself.... Letting go I suppose...

Dom: Yes, that's what it is about. You are not the ego, so dropping the ego, letting go, surrendering....still leaves awareness, leaves simplicity, brings one back to being like a child pre-programming, pre-ego.

Hayley: I've been getting up an hour earlier for work to meditate, and any spare time I have around day to day life I dedicate to being still, in awareness, and it's changing my life in every way. So simple yet so rewarding.

Dom: This is great news!!! This will change everything as well as trigger grace, love, and access to soul, ego death, Holy Spirit, etc. Keep going with this.

Hayley: When in awareness I feel an intense warmth, overwhelming love, and comforting peace, it really is so so beautiful...

Dom: Great, yes it makes all sorts of beautiful inner aspects flower and remain permanently.

Hayley: So I guess I really was just wanting your advice on what do I do now/where do I go next?

Dom: Next is a complete detachment and seeing through the ego so it falls away. Next is to read the book I've attached. Leave everything else alone for now, besides the awareness practice, and put all energy into reading the book attached and applying each chapter to yourself, to seeing the things written there in your own reality. Done right, it will open up access to Union. So it's reading the attached book + lots of surrender, letting go of the ego and all the illusions will lead to Union.

Hayley: Do I just carry on and continue with awareness, prayers and meditation to be closer to and deepen my union God?

Dom: Read the attached book and apply it. E-mail if you have questions.

Hayley: How do I completely let go of/see through the ego? Is the ego just your negative thoughts? How do I know when it's real, I follow my heart, not my head right? (Sorry for all the questions!) I'm a little unsure where I'm at in my growth and where to go from here, if you could guide me a tad that would be brill.

Dom: Read the attachment it will all make it clear and if it isn't, then e-mail back for more clarity. The Ego isn't you, so let go of any notion or feeling that there is a "you."

Instead of "I am reading this e-mail," it should be replaced with the sense/seeing/feeling that "Reading this email is happening on its own."

Instead of "I am hearing sounds," it should be replaced with "Hearing is happening all on its own." or "Hearing is happening and there is no hearer."

Instead of "I am seeing," it should be replaced with the sense/seeing/feeling that "Seeing is happening and there is no seer."

Instead of "I am thinking thoughts," it should be replaced with the sense/seeing/feeling that "thoughts are occurring and there is no thinker"

Instead of "I am Aware," it should be replaced with the sense/seeing/feeling that "Awareness is aware'ing without an Aware'er."

Instead of "I am breathing," it should be replaced with the sense/seeing/feeling that "Breathing is happening on its own without a breather."

Apply the above formula to everything you think and feel to be "you" and apply the sense/seeing/feeling that there is no you in all things throughout the day. Work, talking to others, meditation, walking, eating, peeing, showering, going to sleep, waking up in the a.m., going to sleep in the p.m., teeth brushing.....all actions are happening on their own with no you in any of it.

Also read the attachments and continue gently with awareness + surrender + letting go.

Check back in if there are questions.

Hayley: Thanks Dom, will do! :)

Note* At this point the intuitive sense was right from the first two books I sent her. They gave her the background on what the ego is and how it operates, and revealed to her how Awareness is the 'Seeing/Perceiving', however the mix up was in the practices given in those books where there is still a 'You' that has to develop more Awareness. I quickly saw through the hang up and sent her some more material, a collection of exchanges showing others working out the seeing through of illusion based identity. After receiving it all, it took about six days for her to reply with the first vital experiential 'Seeing' through the illusions.

Hayley: Hi Dom

Another fab book, thank you again. Hallelujah, I am finally there, through the gate!! It was so obvious.... And crikey what a relief it is to finally get rid of that weight off my shoulders. I didn't know whether to lmfao or weep when the realization came to me!!! So unbelievably simple. Nothing has changed, but everything has changed, the BS is gone and it's all so simple and clear....life is just flowing by, thoughts come and go...freedom... Bliss.. everything just IS !!!

Dom: I was wondering if you can give more details here on how the shiftless shift happened, where were you, what were you doing, how did it go about, feelings, thoughts, atmosphere, place, etc.

Hayley: Union for me was a gradual process. The first breakthrough came when I started making and taking time out every day to be still, go within and meditate on God. These were the first steps. Then He began to reveal Himself to me. Occasionally I get pulled out. It's incredible :) The first initial OBE was unbelievable. I feel very blessed to have been given that precious gift.

My thoughts and mantra whilst in this zone would be 'of God', ranging from biblical verses (I am the way, truth and life, I am with you in the stillness etc), to Jesus Prayer and also words like 'Love', 'Trust', 'Truth', that kind of thing, I repeat in my head whilst breathing , surrendering and focusing on Him.

Usually at home, laid out on my bed like a starfish!(I don't like to have anything like legs or arms crossed, as I feel it blocks flow of energy lol!!) When I made this time and effort is when things really started progressing for me spiritually. I get 'rushes' of intense warmth, tingling and love, I could feel Their presence in and around me. So amazingly beautiful, as you know :) I would and still do wake up an hour earlier before I start my day, and always at night. I find now if I don't have my time with Him in the morning especially, I feel really 'off' all day. I tend to try and BE and go within In the same place, as I feel the space then takes on that energy, and I instantly feel connected, it's my sanctuary, although it can be done anywhere, if the need arises.

Dom: Also, did any fear arise and if so how was it dealt with. (many of the people I work with, when they get to the fear part of the ego's deconstruction and illusion, tend to back away and get scared, so if there were any experiences of fear that manifested around the shift(s), how was fear handled/dealt with?

Hayley: Yes of course, as with the unknown there is naturally a hesitation and a need to back off and stay in your safe, known, familiar bubble. There was definitely a nervy sense when I started to break through. There were definitely feelings of 'awe', a kind of ' no going back from this' feeling, which was scary, but I just trusted....

To be honest, ditching the illusion, self and Ego, was a welcomed relief, I don't know, with everything that had been going on personally with me and with my situation as it was, I was quite keen and eager to step away, it was a risk I was willing to take!

So maybe I was fearless going into this, I'm not sure? A kind of 'what do I have to lose attitude'?

Dom: Yeah, there was a feeling that arose on this end, something to the extent of "Hayley broke through" and then the email today, makes sense.

Okay, so now there needs to be sitting with this (without the 'you' sitting) so that everything deeply sinks in. Being!!!! Being with/as the flow, with/as the bliss. Seeing is happening without a seer, hearing is happening without a hearer, thinking is happening without a thinker, awareness is aware without an awarer, and the cherry on top is this = A full and utter existential surrender and letting go!!! Got it? To reiterate:

A full and utter existential surrender and letting go!!!

Yes, there is no you to let go or surrender....but physically surrender/letting go of body identification, of all tension, any knots, any additional "stuff" that's coming up is coming up for the purpose of spring cleaning. A full and utter surrender and letting go.

And that leaves everything as it is, the Isness is God. But sitting with this (without a sitter) still has to happen in time so everything deepens, stabilization, knowing this, feeling this, being this.

Not sure if you watched a vid I made on my channel:

https://www.youtube.com/watch?v=uj6UjdJV1Bg

That vid will now be entirely comprehended, whereas if there was a watching it before, it was only maybe hinted or intuited. The Isness is Omnipresent.

So all that's left is really a deepening of the Isness, of flow, of Water (God is the Ocean of Isness), of bliss, of surrender, of letting go, of not just no Identifying with the mind (which is just illusions) but also with the body (which is just an appearance in Isness.)

The Ego will fall away, in time, and this will be Ego death (everything Christ referred to, Die to the Self and take up thy cross, I and Father are One, the Kingdom is within, etc)

Welcome to Union (even though there is no you to welcome, lol ;)

Hayley: Ahh that's so cool, you knew, love that!!

So I actually really do just wanna let this all sink in and ride with it for a while, whilst going even deeper in prayer, letting go, awareness etc. This is beyond anything I've ever known or experienced before and it's a little overwhelming. It's hard to even put into words how I'm feeling. Totally overwhelmed, euphoric and saturated in His love, and in love with Him is a start!

'The Isness is God'...
That's SO powerful... So God and I are one... Wow, You just got me there!

Thank you ever such a lot for all of your help so far, it's so kind of you take the time to hold my hand through this, I really appreciate it so much, you are a star!

Will Listen to the link now :)

Note* Sometimes at this stage, any breakthroughs, grace, realizations and so forth can be lost or some confusion can set in that arises from the Ego. So it's usually pretty vital to check in a see if what has been seen or experienced, is permanent or not. So I e-mailed the next day.

Dom: Just a courtesy check...making sure everything is still deepening, revealing, flowing, being.....

the Isness!!!!!

Hayley: Hey Morning,

So glad you've emailed, I had the strangest thing happen to me last night!!
Like an out of body experience...
I have been praying loads and getting deeper and closer, ditching the Ego etc since we last spoke.
(This is tricky to describe, I'll do my best)

I was led in my bed in the stillness/meditating, (I had my eyes open so I know I wasn't dreaming)and I felt something pull me out of myself, I was floating about 2 feet above my body!
I saw a long bright glowing line, almost like when the sunsets and you get that last bit of light, in line with the ocean?!!

Then it happened, I saw/felt Jesus. He was holding my hand. When I tried to reach back out I 'woke up' and it went away. (it probably lasted a minute or so, not long). Afterward was like the biggest bear hug you ever had, all warm cozy, lush.

I've been up all night since lol! X

Note* When the initial breakthrough(s) or realization(s) occur, there are

69

various and different mystical/spiritual manifestations and gifts that arise. Some people can see and experience the heavens, others have so much bliss pouring out of them it affects whoever they come around, while for others it can be very subtle and peaceful process, or in Hayley's case, coming out of the body to witness Christ!

Regardless, these aren't things or experiences to look for or cling to because then there's a possibility of the ego arising all over again and creating a new identity called the "Spiritual Ego" as in, "I'm special because I have these experiences and others don't, I have Union, but others don't, and so on. Also, these experiences, if they do come, manifest in the form of Grace, as gifts, and they come when the false identity is out of the way and surrendered. So I nonchalantly reminded Hayley of this in the next reply:

Dom: Great!!! So a mystical experience, out of body, all these things that a Christian Mystic should be experiencing and going through, this is all great. Get used to it because it will be like this from now on, plus continuing to Be, to sit with the deepening of all these things, with the fact that there is no "you", allowance, flow, love, openness, happiness. Love!!!!

Hayley: Really! OMG!!! My first mystical experience ... Wow..! Honestly Dom, thanks for confirming, as I've been up half of the night, and all day today feeling/thinking about it, I'm exhausted!! How did u realize/handle your first experience?

Dom: Get used to them. They are part of what we are supposed to experience when unraveling Union, ego death, accessing Christ, etc. They are part of a Spiritual Life and there will be more.

Hayley: Why did that happen? Why did my body and mind get/ receive/feel/ see that?

Dom: Because when there is no more ego (deny thyself and take up thy cross) then there is access to Union, Spirit realms, Soul/Spirit, Christ, etc on a deeper mystically profound level.

Hayley: Whooahh what's next lol!!

Dom: A continuation of non ego identification in all situations, while driving, working, talking to others, eating, walking, cooking......no 'I' in all situations as well as sitting (meditation) daily to allow all of this to deeply sink in, so it is all embodied and stabilized.

Allowing is happening, life is happening, surrender and letting go are happening, meditation is happening, but nobody is doing these things...which are all just happening on their own, yes?

(A few weeks later Hayley would respond, and the expression of so much Mystical Love became self evident through the words)

Hayley: Hi So I just really wanted to let you know, and thank you so much for everything Dom, getting me there, your time, your patience, support and books!!
You're a fabulous teacher.. ...this wouldn't have ever happened without you, and your guidance ..You truly are an angel...(You were right about the mystical experiences too, there have been more)! Life will never be the same again, it's all just happening, being! bless you :)

Dom: This is great...... this is what Christ was alluding to, is this rebirth/awakening that has happened in your life. Just keep the undoing going until Union is permanent, stabilized, and embodied through all daily experience!!!

And Love too! Allowing Love to flower in the heart towards all things, all people, is another deeper level to all of this. Love for Love's sake!

This is great! It's a blessing to hear all of this. Just keep allowing, unraveling, and sharing these kinds of things with others, as I do as well. Then the whole world will change! So much Love for you!

Hayley: I know! It's all so amazing! It feels like going from 0 -100 mph, and stepping into a new dimension, like everything I'm seeing/living/feeling is in HD! I feel completed detached from things, situations, life, but also have never felt more alive! It brings love and joy to the soul, exciting! Everything now is getting SO much deeper, intense, overwhelming it really is incredible that my being can be this close to Him, it makes me wanna cry!(with love) Blessings and lots love to you too my friend

Note* (A few weeks later, I would check in on her again)

Dom: Hey, just a courtesy check to see how is everything unraveling. Just a reminder, the path, love, flow, acceptance, non-resistance, Christhood...all these things continue to deepen....there is no end...... just take heed that there are no old identifications re-looping themselves in the mind......there is a spring cleaning going now, so allow all things to fall away so that only God remains. From the profound depths of Union and Love, Dom.

Hayley: Hello! Ah bless you, you're so thoughtful, great to hear from you.

All is unraveling well, the realization of what I've been so hungry and craving for is here, is so humbling. God is revealing himself to me and it's just so gorgeous! It feels incredibly personal, like it's just Us.

The initial 'high' has now leveled out, and I'm going with the flow of things, absorbing everything daily, praying, meditating, everything's happening, being. I have the most random urges to pray, like during the night when I'm sleeping, like at 2, or 3, or 4 o'clock in morning, I get woken up and I just HAVE to pray, it's like we're having a conversation, this happens most nights, lol!!

However, one thing that hasn't leveled is the intense amount of Love I get/feel, is through the roof! When I think it can't, it just gets better and better, so much Love!

Although I sometimes struggle with the ego, which tries to creep in though, but I'm aware of it, and keep focused, reminding myself there is no me, so I guess within time that will fade? Like you say, "spring cleaning." Mystical experiences are happening more too, which as you know are so cool :) So all in all life is sweet!

Lots of love to you
Hay x

Ps .Do you ever have dreams of dark forces?
I had a strange one the other day, it's playing on my mind...

Dom: Sounds great! So everything that's going on, on your end is just the deepening, spring cleaning, more Union etc. It's a journey with no journeyer...

Spontaneous prayer is great, it's just pure Love communing with God, a personal relationship that's flowering and bliss for God arising, perfectly normal on the mystical path.

The ego will fade with time and drop out completely as long as there is a permanently established "Seeing" that "It" isn't who you are, that "It" is false and illusory. This "Seeing" has to be established daily and through all situations, else the egotism will find a variety of ways to creep back in, in a variety of situations like with co-workers, clients, family, traffic, not liking something, preferences, etc.....so to destroy all those things means to see that none of them are you and they are all daydreamed beliefs that can be constantly let go of and surrendered...and this will eventually bring about an egoless stillness.

With dark forces.....yes there are such things. Just like people, there are good ones and bad ones that play out through the ego. Also, all around us is a spiritual realm with varieties of beings, souls, angels/demons, etc..... so learn to be fearless in the face of all that is around and casting anything negative out your life, home, body, dreams, etc is as simple as "I cast out all dark forces in the name of Jesus Christ of Nazareth." I also routinely sage all walls/doors/windows/corners of my house and car with sage and holy water while praying the name of Christ over it all as forms of protection, do some of that and you will be in Christ's hands of protection.

Note* (I would again, check in with her roughly two months later)

Dom: Hey, everything good? Things still deepening? Flow, openness, oneness.....?

Hayley: Hey Dom. It's weird, since sage-ing my salon, car and house like you suggested, things instantly started to flow better, like a blockage has been swept away! Things are still unraveling nicely, oneness, praying, letting go, ego falling away, contemplation and devotions etc,
It's all still so absolutely stunning...

I'm finding there so much patience, peace and love (for everything/everyone), I'm so chilled out, nothing bothers me! Do you know what I mean?

Dom: Yes of course I know. These things will continue to deepen, the gifts of the Spirit. It makes me sometimes even ask how was I able to function prior to being taken apart and put back together by God.

Hayley: I'm reading and studying theology books, which are very interesting...
This mysticism/spiritual growth, is heavy stuff huh!?! :-)

Dom: Yes it is heavy. You might want to be careful with too much of that because book knowledge is not the direct experience of God. It is merely theoretical suppositions of other people's experiences and claims, so what happens many times when people read that material is they come across a description of an experience, and then guess what the false illusion ego (I-Thought) says: "I want that, what do I have to do to get that and I won't be happy until I achieve that." And right there in the false sentence, there is the folly, the trap, the division and illusion.

Granted the heart longs for the things of God, however God is Unity, and Love, and patience, and peace, everywhere and in all things as you have experienced and hopefully continue to do so.

Just wanted to ask you so I can close out the exchange for the book, is there anything you wanted to mention in terms of the changes and the ongoing process? Perhaps words of wisdom to others based on your go at this whole process? Maybe even some insights and intuitions in terms of what you feel would be the beneficial continuation of your own path in Union? Can you tell me where you are now? What do you see is important to this whole process? Continually stabilizing Union? Integrating it in the rest of life?

Hayley: So now for me there's daily connection, and a deeper, closer relationship evolving. Union is stabilized, flowing and unfolding in day to day life, but making time to Be is essential. My life has completely changed. I have more patience, love, my intuition is sharp, premonitions, inner peace, awareness, the gifts are endless. Tbh, I'm not sure myself what the next step on this path is taking me, it's all still fairly new to me too, I'm just going with the flow, it's all just happening!

Dom: Do you notice what tends to pull you out of Union?

Hayley: It's totally random, and has only happened a few times for me. I'm usually in deep prayer/meditation when it comes about. I'm very much in the zone and surrendering, and then when in this oneness, like my soul is leaving my body. It doesn't last very long, just glimpses, a minute, if that. The awareness is there. I have no control over it.

Dom: Is there a continuation of letting go of the rest of the stuff of the ego/mind, past
hurts, past traumas, forgiveness, etc?

Hayley: Yes, it does take some effort, as with my job I can get distracted with the conversations and chit chat I have with my clients, and egotism can work its way back in. Personally I have let go of all of the past dramas for my own sanity! (Even though there is no me)! Forgiveness is never easy, but I'm learning it's always the best option in the long run!

Dom: And what would you recommend to others as they're going through their
own process in their own path of seeing through and letting go of all
the false illusions of I/Me/Mine-Ego construct?

Hayley: So I would say, it's essential to make the time daily to BE and go within. Once you have 'seen' the illusion, everything starts to unfold beautifully. Everything changes, but nothing changes, it just all happens. Seeing is believing, you have to see it! The main thing is to just be aware, open your heart, trust, and all will be revealed... Expect the unexpected!

***

CHAPTER 4

EMMA'S EXCHANGE

After finding my videos and sending a brief introduction, I sent Emma four exchanges that were completed and were the primary four that were proving to be sufficient for most people to get this whole Union business. Particularly useful to her was Adam's exchange from which one can extract a set of practices with all of this, and the supporting YouTube/MP3 meditations I started providing to people to use as pointers.

However, even after reading all the exchanges, Emma still needed simplicity of the practices being extracted and laid out specific to her in a question and answer format. Eventually during the exchange, a myriad of emotional releases begin to rise up before Union begin to manifest all on its own. Below is the exchange as follows over the course of a few months.

Emma: Hi Dom, so I'm starting to make my way through the exchanges and this is all very serious stuff and makes complete sense to me. It's a bit scary to be quite honest but I feel like for myself it's revolutionary. I can really relate to what I've read so far and I'm really sick and tired of all this identity crap, sick and tired of having to be who I am based on what others think. Society, family, all my past relationships and past hurts, it's almost a relief but also I feel some tension with all of this like if I start letting go, I will lose myself and then what? Does that make sense? Anyhow, I'm still reading and re-reading some parts and will get back to you soon. Thanks for everything, really a breath of fresh air!

Dom: Hey Emma, of course this is serious because if there is a heartfelt calling for experiential Union, to real know via experience what Union is like, these are powerful blueprints that dozens have successfully gone through and undone themselves with this process, and what's waiting on the other side after this is finished, is better than living an illusory life of egotism and falsehood.

When you say its 'scary' is that something that is permanent? When did 'scary' arise and why? Give these questions a go and answer truthfully. What was the scariest for myself and others when they started down this path, is to live the remainder of life wrapped entirely in the fiction and mental slavery of the delusional day dreaming of the ego, so then is there really anything to be scared of at this point other than being enslaved for the rest of one's life? You seem to already understand being sick and tired living this identified life, that's why there was the initial seeking on YouTube for videos and initial e-mail correct? Tell me why did you seek out any vids and eventually e-mail me?

There is nothing to worry about losing One's self because when that is lost, God is found, make sense? Can you also tell me which exchanges you read so far?

Emma: Yeah, it's all making much more sense; at least on the intellectual level 'I' seem to get it. Scary isn't permanent, it's just my reaction from reading these exchanges and I guess sort of intuiting where all this work is going in losing myself to Union. I see what you mean about living the rest of life mired in egotism, it is pretty scary to carry in that way and I guess I can say, that's why I contacted you and was seeking online, it's like an inner sense that there is more, something deeper and genuine is there with the experiences expressed in Mysticism, but not knowing how to access or unlock what was being intuited or what is in these exchanges so far. The more I read the more they make sense though.

And church is great and everything but for me it's just not enough, I can't really open up to anyone there about my past and issues for fear of being judged, and what will anyone think about me crying in a prayer group, expressing my regrets and mistakes, and dwelling on the past. I don't know, I just don't feel comfortable opening up to people, but with God I can and there's still that inner need for something more, make sense?

So far I read Hayley, Adam, and just started on Michael. I know you gave me an order in which to read them, but I started reading on my phone on the way to work in a carpool where there is a lot of talking going on and lost track of order.

Dom: Okay, so getting all of this on the intellectual level is important because it precludes having an understanding of all of this, but then this has to be directly applied via direct experience. In the Adam exchange that you read, there is a set of practices, can you start applying those? On my YouTube page it's basically three videos; A.M. Meditation, P.M. Meditation, and Atmosphere of No Self Meditation.

Also with the whole 'scary' thing, it's just an emotion arising and there are 2 choices with anything that arises based on emotions, thoughts, reactions, etc:

1. Identify with it
2. Don't identify with it

So returning to all of this being a bit 'scary' can you return to that feeling and tell me what is it like? Can you tell me if this is true that there are two choices there? There is a choice in which you can either identify with this 'scary' or not identify with it?

Emma: Yeah I read the Adam exchange, but there's just so much there, and between reading that, and now I'm halfway through Michael's exchange, and work, and getting dinner ready and lunch for the next day, I just try to read whenever there is time and just before going to sleep, so it's a bit sporadic and mixed in with all the other stuff.

I went back into the 'scary' feeling and it's so strange this whole thing about having a choice not to identify with it. It's definitely there if I think about losing myself, and what is Union like, and fearing it a bit, it almost doesn't make sense that I have a choice not to identify with it, like I have to because it belongs to me and it's my emotion. But the thing is you're right that it's not always there and only comes up if I explore it or if I associate thoughts of the unknown that it comes back up. I'm still working with this choice thing and so far it's really not so clear.

Can you clarify the practices from Adam's exchange so I can put them to use?

Dom: Yeah, I'll get to Adam's exchange in a second, first I want to clarify choice with identifying or not identifying. I want you to use your imagination and think of a blackened rotten banana with fruit flies all over it. Just picture it in your imagination and you can even imagine how bad this rotting piece of fruit smells.

Now look and see that there are choices there, which are to keep on imagining this gross disgusting rotting fruit that is ready for garbage and is stinking up the place, or there is a choice to no longer imagine this and let go of it, especially since it's not necessarily a pleasant thought to have. Do you see this?

Emma: Yeah, I just did it and I see your point. It's repulsive to think of that and I don't really want to keep imagining something so yucky, so I don't keep it there long and let it go in order to write you back.

Dom: Yeah, see, that's it right there, you just had a direct experience of the choice to identify with this imagined banana, and then to let it go and no longer identify with it. So see if you can do this with 'scary', because 'scary' is also in sense, unpleasant for it to be there and to have. Can you do this?

Emma: Yeah, I see your point now, but it's a lot harder with emotions and will take some practice. So this is what you're alluding to in Adam's exchange with the practices? Can you break it all down for me again so I can ask questions?

Dom: Sure, let's do it experientially right now. Can you tell me how do you experience life right now in this exact moment? How is reality experienced?

Emma: Hmm, there is a lot there to write about. All the things I've been through, my whole past, experiences with parents, growing up, different stages of adolescence, various experiences with people in my life, school, vacations, sights, sounds, food, being sick, sometimes healthy, teenage years, first boyfriend, losing my grandmother who I loved, lots of different emotions, sometimes confusion, figuring out life, trying to be a good person, a Christian, there is just so much there. Do you want me to keep going and make a list?

Dom: Actually, I just want you to talk about just right now, this present moment. All those things that happened in the past, they're all done now, they are in the past and gone. Everything that is hoped for in the future isn't here yet, so we won't worry about the future either, so let's just write about the present moment without going into the past or the future. What is the experience of the present moment like, describe that. Are there senses? Emotions? Thoughts? Ideas? Pain? Comfort? Go into it.

Emma: Oh okay, I see what you mean. I'm just sitting here after work, full from dinner with a cup of hot chocolate and a cookie for dessert. I'm sitting on my favorite place on the couch with a blanket and the laptop on my lap. It's starting to lightly snow outside and the snowflakes really get lit up when they fall past the street lights illuminating everything. I love how it's all Christmas-y this time of the year. I'm a bit excited to be replying regarding all of this and trying to figure out this Union thing, so there is a sense of excitement and wondering how this will all happen and if it's really even possible. I guess I'm still scared with some anxiousness, but I remember you saying that I have choice whether to identify with it or not, and no I'm not going to think about that nasty banana or it will ruin my desert, lol. I'm also a bit sleepy and might take a nap after the desert because it's just so comfortable here. Is that good so far?

Dom: Yes, that's plenty. So let's break all that down. So if you ask yourself "How am I currently experiencing life?" There will be all of the following: Sights, sounds, smells, (all the senses) feelings, emotions, a body, and thoughts. Is this correct? Am I missing anything from this list? Can you check again to see how you are currently experiencing life and see if all those are there and if I'm missing anything?

Emma: Yeah, I'm just going to check and type as they all come. The feeling of the keyboard by the fingers, the TV is on in the background with the volume set to low, the smell of the hot chocolate, the feeling of being warmly wrapped up in my blanket, seeing the screen as I type, feeling full from the food and sleepy, excited about figuring this all out, looking to see if I'm missing anything. I think that's it, I think you named all that is there.

Dom: Okay, so let's take another step with all of this. Are you also aware of the fingers typing? Aware of eyes seeing, aware of the nose smelling the hot chocolate, aware of the ears hearing the background of the TV, aware of the fullness/sleepiness in the body, aware of the excitement of trying figure this all out?

Emma: Yes, but this is a bit trippy to do, it's almost like messing with my brain but I think I see what you're getting at. When I become aware of the smell of the chocolate, it's like there is something more there now. Usually I would just smell the hot chocolate and be happy about it and want to drink it, but now being aware of smelling is sort of spacey and strange. Same thing when I go to the other senses.

Dom: Can you be aware of the feeling of being excited about all of this as well?

Emma: Yeah, that's pretty easy, it's just like being aware that 'scary' was there when you asked me about it a while back, but now when I become aware, the excitement is there, it seems like there is more space there, it's hard to describe and it's very subtle.

Dom: Good, this is a good start. So remember when I was replying to Adam about micro-events? This is what you do throughout the day, just kind of have a pause and ask. 'What is the experience of the present moment like, what's going on right now?' And then you just check and see what's going on by scanning through the senses, the thoughts, emotions, feelings, the body, etc.

Only now I want you to see what that's like by surrendering any identifications that might be there. So now it's going to get a bit deeper and harder, but with time and practice you will pick up on it.

So what I want you to do is again find a place to sit and go through the senses one by one, and we will start with seeing. We will first breakdown seeing and then write back so that I know you got it.

So where ever you are sitting, just see with your eyes whatever is there. Since it's winter there, most likely it's in a room, and there are walls, rugs, a floor, ceiling, walls, windows, etc. So just see, look at everything and see that while there are all types of details in that room, they all makeup the one room. Just spend a few minutes familiarizing yourself what it's like to see, what it's like to use the eyes to look around and see different things, details, see the whole room at once, what the eyes themselves feel like, resting gently in the eye sockets in the face and having the ability to look in different directions, to focus on one thing, or to focus on several things all at once.

After those few minutes are up, now switch to just allowing seeing to take place all on its own. Just allowing seeing to Be as it is. Allowing seeing to be effortless, so there is no need to strain, or to force anything, or to look for anything specific, or to seek, or to wander, just letting go of seeing so it's nice and relaxed and effortless.

Spend a good 5-10 minutes like this, effortless seeing, relaxed, surrendered seeing, allowing seeing to take place all on its own, seeing happening without a seer..

Then when you are done, can you report back here and tell me what you find? Can you describe what this was like and what the differences were between being aware of seeing, looking around, using the eyes vs. the latter which was effortless seeing, surrendered, allowing seeing to happen on its own without being identifying with it?

Emma: Hey Dom, yeah I'm back. This time I did it on my bed with a pillow propped up for my back and a blanket to keep my legs warm. Did as you suggested and it was pretty cool. In the beginning when I was getting used to seeing in my bedroom, it was more effort, more doing, like forced seeing, and looking around, and wondering what's the point of this, and lots of thoughts, and that excited feeling was there too almost like if I was going to see something mystical.

Becoming aware of seeing added that spaciousness to it all, it's still all so strange and new to me all of this, but there is definitely something different I can feel, almost like I'm learning about life all over again.

Then when I switched to allowing seeing to happen on its own, getting used to that effortless seeing, it was strange as well. My body loosened, there was lots of physical relaxation, everything was simple and easy, but there were still a lot of thoughts about different things like "Am I doing this right, what's the point, what am I looking for, has it been 5 minutes yet, I still have to make lunch for tomorrow," and just really non-stop thoughts. Also that feeling of excitement, of looking for something to happen was there.

Dom: Hey Emma, good descriptors, there's a lot there to work with. Ultimately what you're doing here is to see that the process of 'Eye's seeing' is happening all by itself and it doesn't require any effort or any 'you' in order for seeing to happen, naked seeing without identifying with it, without adding any thoughts that 'I am seeing." Then you start applying this to all of the senses, all of experience.

So in a sense, it's letting go of seership, letting go of thinking that you are the one who is seeing, letting go of a believe that there is a Seer in the first place, and getting used to this sense that Seeing is happening all on its own.

Does this make sense?

Emma: Yeah, I get it now; it's just like in the other exchanges. I'm still a bit confused though because even when I just let seeing happen on its own, there are still all these thoughts about it, like if I'm doing it right and how much longer and the incessant thoughts about it all keep going.

Dom: That's fine; you're just new to this so it will take some practice and getting used to. So let's get to the next part of this. Can you answer me the following? What do eyes do? What do ears do? What does the nose do? What do thoughts do? What does Awareness do?

Emma: My eyes can see, can look around, focus, take in various details, see far or close. My ears hear. My nose smells and when I breathe it can happen through my nose or mouth. My thoughts, that's a bit tricky and I'll have to have a better look there before answering. My awareness is also tricky, it's aware or can be aware of different things like we did in the practice before. So I can switch from being aware of the eyes seeing then switch to the ears hearing, then to the nose smelling.

Dom: That's okay if some things are a bit tricky; we will dissect everything and make it all clear. What I forgot to mention, is that I wanted you to answer the question without using 'I, my, mine, me,' etc. But we can break that down now.

So with eyes seeing, can you look just at the eyes without adding the idea that they are your eyes? Can you look at the eyes objectively, nakedly, in a manner without adding any identity? So what I am asking you to do is to be aware of the eyes seeing; and feel, see, be aware of them in a way as if they

84

are happening all on their own, they don't belong to you or anyone else, seeing is just its own thing that's happening all on its own regardless of any beliefs, thoughts ideas, identities, ownership?

Also, what's happening prior to what? Is seeing happening prior to thoughts occurring, or thoughts occurring prior to seeing? Is the thought, "I am seeing" required for "seeing to occur, or does seeing occur regardless of what thoughts are occurring?

Emma: Yeah it's all starting to come together between reading the exchanges and playing with all these perspectives, I think I see what you're getting at, pun intended ;) Yeah, in a way seeing is happening all on its own but there is such a strong urge to label it as me, or to feel that I'm the one who's seeing I guess if I start messing with these different perspectives it gets a bit easier to see it that way, seeing happening all on its own.

As far as priority, if I become aware of seeing first, then it seems like seeing is prior to thoughts. And if I become aware of thoughts, it seems like they are prior to seeing, but none of that makes sense, because they happen at the same time. So if I'm aware of seeing, it's occurring regardless of whether or not I'm aware of any thoughts taking place, and if I'm aware of thoughts, then seeing is happening regardless. I guess it's all going on at the same time would be my best answer. And no, I don't have to think about seeing for seeing to happen.

Dom: Okay, good, so just like in the other exchanges, you start doing the same thing you did with seeing, but with everything else, hearing, smelling breathing, sitting, **thoughts/thinking**, awareness, etc.

Technically it's extracting, or letting go of any identity from any of these things that are always taking place in experience any time you check and ask, "How am I currently experiencing reality? Only from now on, what you're going to do is remove the 'I', so it becomes, "How is experience experiencing itself in this present moment? By removing the 'I', I mean to no longer believe in that idea, no longer believe in it as a label, as who you are, seeing it as a daydream and illusion.

So then there is a scanning of all the senses and seeing them as happening all on their own, all effortless, all relaxed, all surrendered, all let go of one

85

by one and resting in that state which from now on I will call the "Atmosphere of No Self".

So you set aside half an hour to start, every day no excuses, because excuses will just be from the ego, justifying a variety of ways to not go through with this, to prevent Union, to make up stuff, to make irrelevant little things seem much more important than going through with this so just be aware of the excuses and let go of them so this is put into practice. Believe me out of all the e-mails and people I work with in person, the ego creates a ton of illusory rationalizations in order to defeat the seeing of its own unreality.

Here's how it would look:

Find a comfortable semi-quiet place with little distractions as a primary location for sitting to allow this atmosphere of no-self to be established. Later you can start doing it with busy and chaotic places like train stations, outside near a schoolyard, near traffic, at a family gathering and so on.

Sit in a comfortable position and be aware of eyes seeing for a few minutes, then allow seeing to occur all on its own. Effortless seeing all happening on its own, it doesn't require a you to do what it does, seeing is relaxed, is surrendered, there is no 'you' who is seeing, it's just happening all on its own, effortless and simple. Allow seeing to be like that for a good 5 minutes, then move on to hearing. When there's a getting the hang of it, move on from 'seeing happening on its own" after 30 seconds to a minute, and on to the next sense.

Be aware of ears hearing for a few minutes, and then allow hearing to occur all on its own. Effortless hearing all happening on its own, it doesn't require a you to do what it does, hearing is relaxed, is surrendered, there is no 'you' who is hearing, it's just happening all on its own, effortless and simple. Allow hearing to be like that for a good 5 minutes, then moving on to breathing.

Be aware of breathing for a few minutes, and then allow breathing to occur all on its own. Effortless breathing all happening on its own, it doesn't require a you to do what it does, breathing is relaxed, is surrendered, there is no 'you' who is breathing, it's just happening all on its own, effortless and simple. Allow breathing to be like that for a good 5 minutes, then moving on to the body as a whole.

Be aware of the entire body for a few minutes, and then allow the body to occur all on its own. Effortless bodying all happening on its own, it doesn't require a you to do what it does, the body is relaxed, is surrendered, there is no 'you' who is bodying, it's just happening all on its own, effortless and simple. Allow the body to be like that for a good 5 minutes, then moving to thoughts.

Be aware of thoughts for a few minutes. The content of the thoughts will be about all sorts of subjects, i.e. "am I doing this right, what time is it, how much longer, where is Union, what's the point, I should just give up, yesterday was a bad day, tomorrow might also be bad, maybe good but who knows, I hate my job, life is pointless, when will my ego become unglued," and so on and so forth.

Just watching these thoughts as they occur, no identifying with any of them, no judgment, no other comments, just a simple watching, awareness of them, and then allowing thoughts to occur all on their own. Effortlessly watching thoughts all happening on their own, it doesn't require a 'you' for thoughts to occur, and while they are occurring, the watching of these thoughts is relaxed, is surrendered, there is no 'you' who is having these thoughts, there is no 'you' who is watching them, it's just happening all on its own, effortless and simple. Allow the thoughts to occur like that for a good 5-10 minutes, then moving on to awareness.

Be aware of awareness for a few minutes and then allow awareness to occur all on its own. Effortless awareness all happening on its own, it doesn't require a 'you' to do what it does, the awareness is relaxed, is surrendered, there is no 'you' who is doing the aware part, it's just happening all on its own, effortless and simple. Awareness resting in itself, gently and simply, with no 'you' in any of it. Allow the awareness to be like that for a good 5 minutes, and that makes up the Atmosphere of No Self.

Now when this atmosphere is established, just being as that, resting as that atmosphere of everything as it's happening with no 'you' in any of it. Nothing to look for, nothing to seek, nothing to find, everything surrendered and let go of, and just a simple resting of the atmosphere in the simplicity as it Is.

So I want you to spend time in this atmosphere of No Self so it is established as the baseline of your reality, and give me some descriptions of what it is like there, feelings, moods, insights, experiences, details from the most minute to anything else in between.

Emma: Okay, I think I got it. So just to reiterate before I go into this I'm simply letting go of all 'I-ness, doership, me-ness' from all the factors that make up present moment experience and allowing it all just be that way?

So like you said in the other exchanges, seeing happening without a seer, hearing without a hearer, smelling without a smeller, a body occurring without a bodier, thoughts occurring without a thinker, awareness occurring without and awarer, being without a be'er?

Just remembered that bit from another exchange and it's starting to make sense now.

Dom: Yeah that's it. Very simple, but it has to be applied so that it is put into practice, felt, tasted, understood, experienced, and reported back here so that we can both establish what this No Self Atmosphere is like. Sounds good?

Emma: Hey Dom, yeah it makes sense now and I've been doing it here and there on the way and back from work and lunch break. When I get back home tonight I'll sit in this a bit longer and write back how it was.

Dom: Okay, standing by for the report.

Note* A few days later Emma wrote back

Emma: Okay so just got wrapped up with a session and it was really intense. Lots of stuff coming to the surface, cried a few times, lots of past hurts and regrets bubbling up so I sort of got caught up in the storm of all that. It all came up when there was this deep letting go of everything and just resting like how you described. The thoughts got really rampant and crazy, like a flood of them all chaotic. For a while it was pretty easy to just watch them and let it all be, but eventually all the memories welled up and I started identifying with all of them and that's when the crying started and I just went along with it and let it all out. It was cathartic and really felt like it needed to happen, sort of like it was just waiting for a release I suppose and it just felt good to release all the pent up existential angst. It was like giving everything to God, like if this Union thing is going to happen, at least let me get all this stuff that seems deep within, out of the way so it can happen if it's meant to.

Then there was just more letting go into whatever is there. It seems very simple, peaceful, but the ego won't shut up, always looking for something, wanting to make comments, plans, complaints, and attaching to emotions, to things. It was hard not to identify with the feelings associated with the thoughts, but nevertheless really cool to sit in this atmosphere in this way. I think I'll have to return to this again maybe next time without the crying. It's definitely different and I guess I can say it's also a relief from doing and ego'ing all the time.

Dom: Good job Emma, really happy that you sat with this and yes many of the details you describe about the No Self Atmosphere are true as it is peaceful, still, simple, and so forth, and this is the atmosphere for healing, surrender, letting go, and eventual Union to take place. It's not anything to look for, but these things happen all on their own when there is no 'you' in any of it.

The crying is also good because things will come up from the subconscious while the No Self Atmosphere is established, deepened, sat with longer, allowed to be as it is. So with these subconscious things, what needs to be done is as follows:

See that there is something there, arising, dissect it by figuring out if it's a thought, or an emotion, or an emotion based on a thought, or past hurt, traumatic memories, etc, and just allow that to arise and be there, but without identifying with any of it. Just allowing it to be, with no 'you' in any of it and it will eventually fall away so there is a return to the baseline of the No Self Atmosphere, which is like the sky, and these things that arise are like clouds passing by. Do you understand?

So it's establishing the No Self Atmosphere as the baseline of experiential reality, resting and allowing that atmosphere to be as it is, and then any sort of distraction, discord, thoughts, emotions, discomfort, etc that arises to try to take away from the peacefulness and ISness of the no self atmosphere, it's then allowed to arise, not identified with, and it will eventually fall away so there is a return to the No Self Atmosphere. Got it? Now can you return to this atmosphere again and report back what it is like the second time around? This time allow the atmosphere to be surrendered into in the manner described, for 40 minutes or longer.

Emma: Hey Dom, yeah it makes complete sense. So if crying or anything else was to arise just allow it and let it out, and then return to the baseline right? Also what about the torrent of chaotic thoughts?

Dom: Yeah, if any crying needs to be released, or a sigh of relief, or sleep starts taking over or whatever, just allow it but without identifying with it so that after it passes there is a return to the baseline of seeing that all the senses are happening on their own with no 'you' in any of them, a body without a bodier, breathing happening without a breather, thoughts occurring without a thinker, awareness is aware'ing without an awarer. Got it?

As for the chaotic thoughts, just allowing them to be chaotic without any identifications with them. See that even when thoughts are occurring chaotically, what else makes up the no self atmosphere? Seeing is still happening with no seer, hearing is still there with no hearer, breathing with no breather, awareness with no awarer, and so on, all occurring at the same time as the chaotic thoughts. So just allowing that chaos to be there, it's happening all on its own, there is no chaotic thinker, it's not happening to a 'you,' it's just a part of everything that 'IS' all occurring at the same time as part of the experience of reality, without an experiencer.

These chaotic thoughts are like the death throes of illusion, of something that isn't you, of something that's undergoing the process of becoming unglued. Typical reality for a person is to be completely identified with thoughts. Egotism, daydreaming about the past or the future, selfishness, me me me, I I I, and so on, and now there is a breaking up of those habitual tendencies by sitting in an atmosphere where there is no you to whom these thoughts are happening, and there is no you for these thoughts to attach to, or any place for these thoughts to be identified with, and so they are behaving like a chaotic spoiled child crying and wanting to be the center of attention, but not getting it. Understood? The ego is a make believe spoiled child trying to get attention, trying to steal attention all to its imaginary self, when attention is supposed to be resting in itself without any identifications.

The center of attention in the Atmosphere of No Self is everything all happening all at once with no you in any of it, and everything is loose, surrendered, let go of, and resting as that atmosphere. That chaos will eventually calm down and become simplified as there is this ungluing of believing in anything the ego creates in terms of illusions.

Emma: Hey Dom, makes complete sense. I will have a busy few days; or rather a busy few days will be occurring so there won't be any opportunities to sit as this atmosphere until Saturday for the full 40+ minutes. But I do have a question. Having done this now in short spurts here and there I think I'm beginning to get a feel for this. Is this exactly how the A.M. and P.M. practices go, it's basically just what you described so far right? Because I've been setting my alarm 20 minutes early to establish the atmosphere in the morning as the first thing I do, or rather undo, and just want to make sure this is the same thing I'd undo by going to sleep at night.

Also there is a strong attachment to facebook, texting, and all the social media stuff. I think you mentioned taking a break from all of them right?

Dom: Yes, facebook is basically the digital ego. I cannot tell you enough how many issues are caused via facebook by the people I have helped guide with this Union work. There are a number of psychological/scientific studies on facebook causing depression, distress, comparing one's self to others on there; the grass is greener on the other side egotistical constructs, keeping up with the joneses, jealousy, hatred, and so forth. People only post the good things about themselves, new cars, new houses, smiles, vacation photos, etc.

But people usually won't admit on their own issues of their egotism, depression, imbalances, the alcoholism, the addictions to porn and gambling, the cheating, lying, stealing, divorces, unhappiness, practically all of it caused by the identification with the ego and the body. So you only see a fake-everything-is-perfect version of everyone on there, and the ego takes that facebook profile and creates assumptions, comparisons, speculations, which create more and more problems.

I know that these days, an account there is required most times for jobs and inner social circles, so by all means have one. However, limit your time there else ego creates a web of identification around social media and Union will never happen.

As for A.M./P.M. practices, yes exactly like I've showed you about establishing this no self atmosphere, that's what needs to be done with the alarm clock set 20 minutes prior to the actual wake up time, and 20 minutes just before going to sleep, so it becomes a solidified aspect of your life as a habitual tendency that is beneficial for undoing all the illusions, with two additional added caveats.

For the A.M. practice, there has to be a seeing that waking up is happening on its own, not that 'I' just woke up. So when waking up happens, immediately the ego will be thinking incessantly, "what time is it, I have to brush my teeth, what will I eat for breakfast, etc." So there is this first initial A.M. awareness of watching right away whatever the mind is saying, and establishing that these thoughts are occurring but there is no thinker, there is no one who they are occurring to, they are just happening on their own, that these thought streams are unreal illusion daydreams. Waking up is happening, but there is no waker upper. And then scanning and establishing this sense and seeing of no self with the rest of the senses, body, awareness, and resting as the No Self Atmosphere.

Same deal as above with the P.M. practice, except that falling asleep will start to occur. So the same thing should be applied to falling asleep, it's something that is occurring, and sleep is starting to happen, but there is no sleeper, sleep is beginning to occur all on its own and there is no sleeper to whom its happening to and then scanning and establishing this sense and seeing of no self with the rest of the senses, body, awareness, and resting as the No Self Atmosphere. Resting in this manner, sleep will still take over the body, the mind, and everything else as it deepens, however there is no identification going on anywhere with any part of the sleep occurrence. This P.M. No Self Atmosphere meditation going into sleep is a very vital part of this process, since this will go deeply into the subconscious and continue the undoing and unraveling process even during deep sleep.

Got it?

Emma: Yeah, got it. Some other experiences have started happening but

I'll write more in length this Saturday after a longer session, and have already set up alarm clocks to put this into practice, thanks, Chow!

Note* Almost a week later, Emma writes back on a Saturday.

Emma: Hey Dom, just writing to report back on the A.M./P.M. practices and just completed a 40 minute session. There are a lot of things going on like for starters everything seems a lot more spacious for some reason. I'm also not reacting to things like I used to do, which I noticed this past week at work, even my co-worker mentioned something about me being a bit spaced out even though I wasn't.

She mentioned something about one of the new accountants and I just didn't care because it really didn't matter, so I was just waiting for her to finish but she was waiting for me to reply with something similar and gossipy to what she said. So I just kind of smiled and mentioned something to wave her off, and that's when she asked if I'm okay and if there's something on my mind. I didn't tell her what it was but it's not that there is something on my mind but that this mind isn't even me! Like I got it intellectually at first, but when she mentioned the new guy, I was detached from it all, and watching the ego, and it was pretty much in a moment of stillness so there wasn't the habitual reaction as always. I still can't stop thinking about that moment.

My husband has also mentioned that there seems to be something different about me but I just gave an excuse about the meditations creating more peace. Still these two examples are showing me that something is changing and people around me have noticed.

Anyway, so I sat for 40 minutes and it was pretty intense. It's almost like I can see where egotism and identification try and stick and try to arise, and so I just do like you told me and try not identifying with it so there is a return to present moment experience with no experiencer. Besides the stillness it's extremely peaceful and it's just simple I guess I can say.

The ego comes in and tries to make things of it, like label it as boring and stupid and there are a ton of excuses it creates not to sit, not to do the AM/PM practices, and looks for ways to get wrapped up in identities. A lot of times I don't catch it until realizing that the 'I' thought, got wrapped up in bunch of thoughts, or sleepiness starts creeping in, so for sure next time I have to eat lighter. When getting wrapped up in the thoughts, I just sort of come back to recreating the atmosphere by going back to seeing that the eyes are seeing on their own with no me, same with hearing, and everything else, and then just rest like that, but eventually the ego just gets me to wrap myself in its stories and it really sucks when attention gets stolen by illusions.

I also noticed that breathing gets deeper and I started also making sure to relax any tension in the body as you mentioned that in another exchange. It feels like the atmosphere of no self is like just being all by itself or being with whatever is, but at the same time there is no be'er is this correct?

Anyhow, I think this is all forming as a habit and I'm still reading the exchanges and rereading whenever there's opportunity to do so. It's quite enjoyable to just be and let go into the atmosphere and I'm having some sort of strange experiences happen here and there but I don't know how to explain them. It's like at times everything is just so simple and there's no point in thinking about anything else except to just be in the simplicity, does this make sense?

Dom: Hey Emma, yes it all makes sense and lots of good things you reported back.

So the experience at work when the co-worker mentioned the new guy and there was this experiential detachment from the ego, that was a direct result of you reading all of these exchanges, sitting in the No Self Atmosphere so its established as a baseline, and doing the same during the A.M./P.M. practices. Eventually that sort of experience will become permanent, where the ego will entirely become unglued and fall away so that there is always this pure transparency and seeing everything naked.

And no, don't worry about the thoughts: "How will I ever be able to live without an ego or react or act or do, and so forth." That's just a fear tactic of the ego to not go through ego death. There will still be the ability to react, do things, live, plan, and everything else that makes up life, but it will all be done from a Union/Oneness, all spontaneous without the need to think about them prior. For example do you have to think "I need to blink my eyes every few seconds!" in order for them to do this? Of course not, because it all happens on its own

Same with planning, say a trip to do a retreat somewhere. Making plans just happens, and while there may be an initial thought before, "I need to plan the trip," before actually planning, in Union it's more intuitive and felt besides just thought. But even planning ahead of time via thought, will become inseparable from infinite Unity, all happening on its own effortlessly.

The breathing getting deep, letting go of physical tension, surrendering anything that arises that tries to cause identity is all part of resting in the No Self Atmosphere and the detailed report was excellent. What I also want you to start establishing, is this light enjoyment that there is no you. Add this loving and simple enjoyment of how easy and effortless it is for reality and existence to be happening all on its own without any requirement for you to be there, that way, any tension that arises physically, any thoughts that try to creep in and create identifications to detract from the enjoyment of there being no you, can be let go of and surrendered so there is always that return to the enjoyment of the no self atmosphere.

Here's the thing, scanning out the identity from all senses, ego/thoughts, body, awareness, then surrendering, allowing, being as that No Self Atmosphere, is the closest thing to Union there is. That atmosphere is like the doorway to Union, in that the less of you there is in any aspect of that experience (in the senses, thoughts, body, emotions, tensions, awareness, etc), the less there are any identifications going on, and the more there is just the simplicity, allowing, being as IS, letting go, surrendering to whatever IS, the more the door to Union starts to open.

So by really enjoying and loving being unraveled and undone in this atmosphere, then it's easier to spot and surrender any identification, attachments, tensions, egotism, and there will be a falling in love with resting at the door to Union, and the things that are loved are the things that the heart wants to spend time with.

Whereas if the ego creates discord with the atmosphere, then it will make excuses to have nothing to do with this, to label it as boring, label it as a waste of time, and that nothing will happen there, and that it's not something to look into, that watching movies is more fun, that spending time on social media ego games has more value, and is more important, and so on. It is here that most people fail, because they end up believing these lies and tactics created by the ego, to no longer examine that the ego isn't even who you are, that it's just a stream of illusions that can be seen and disidentified with, that it isn't even real at all but just consists of daydreams, and to see what happens and what will dawn if this entire fabrication and fiction of the ego is no longer identified with and falls away.

Let me know if this makes sense because it's become a bit wordy with all of that context there, but I'm trying to keep it simple for you as originally requested. So to reiterate with simplicity, you already have an experiential knowledge via practice of how to establish and sit in this No Self Atmosphere, but I also want you to see that it is like sitting at the door to Union, and to also enjoy and fall in love with this sitting at the door to Union, so there will always be this inner pull to continue undoing/unraveling, understood?

Emma: Hi Dom, its good if it's a bit lengthy 'cause I've just been rereading and making sense of it all based on all the experiences so far. Today I had something really big come up after reading your last reply. I've spent all these years, pretty much my whole life up to now, figuring out what my identity is and what that all means, and different phases of it and having invested so much into me and who I am and what that all means, entirely completely involved in this 'I', and now to give it all up after building it up is just so crazy. I had some anxiety come up because of this whole thing and was really physically tense after, but then it dawned on me how it's all just more stories right? And since I've been sitting in the atmosphere, I mean it's so easy and simple, and you were right that we surrender at night when going to sleep because I was really watching it last night, how falling asleep happens. I just let go into it and then eventually it happens. The thoughts slow, the body sinks, and the sleep takes over, but in the no self atmosphere, I'm doing the same except while remaining conscious right?

Also, it's so strange because everyone who knows me, has an ego based story about me as well that they believe right? This sort of insight came after my husband blamed me for losing his keys after we both cleaned the house on Sunday, and he eventually found them in the pocket of one of his sweatshirts in the hamper. He argued with me for a good hour while I helped him look for the keys. I kept having to defend myself because I knew I was right. But in his mind, he created this story that I was the one at fault and stuck with this illusion until he was proven wrong by the reality of proof. So then I realized, everyone I know has their cloud of illusions about me and everyone else they know, and everyone else they will ever meet. So I'm starting to see the difference between living this illusion based life in contrast to the detachment from all those illusions in the no self atmosphere. So was this another insight?

Dom: Hey Emma, yeah that was definitely an insight that came to show you how things are for real. Thing is, you can't really control the illusions of others, because they do what they do and it's not even who they are either, even if they are entirely identified with the stream of day dreams. However, there is some control over your own stream of illusions and continuously no longer identifying with any of it, so that it eventually falls away, hence the ungluing.

You see true reality is already naked, prior to thoughts and identifications, can include thoughts and identifications (as seen in those who have created their clouds of illusions they believe about you), and after those thoughts and identifications pass and fall away, reality as it is, naked, continues to be as it is.

Check next time you eat a meal. The act of eating the meal is happening all on its own and while it's happening, seeing is happening, and smelling is happening, and the lungs are breathing, the ears are hearing, the space in the room is there, the walls exist, the feet are on the floor, the butt is on the chair, all of that IS as it IS. Now while that's going on, that nakedness of reality, check and see what the ego is doing. It's usually rushing about with stories about 'I' and what 'I' have to do today, in the future, what happened yesterday, desires, needs, wants, plus all sorts of emotions added onto the thoughts.

Now if you check and look, the act of seeing, or seeing itself with the eyes, doesn't care what thoughts or emotions are there. The eyes continue to see, and they can see everything all at once, or focus on one detail, or switch between peripheral and focused, and back to peripheral. Now there can be seeing, without labeling anything that's seen, or seeing + labeling everything that's seen. So what we are going for is this naked seeing without the need to label what is seen, and then applying the same to everything else and then surrendering and letting go into whatever is left over when this is done. Most importantly is to do this with the thought process, seeing it as impersonal, illusory, unreal, false, detached from, and no longer identified with.

With the anxiety of surrendering identity, it wasn't there yesterday. In fact it was of no concern until the thoughts arose that this whole unraveling and undoing process is happening to all identification. So the concern itself is also an illusion that was created out of thin air, where there were no concerns before, do you see this? So this concern, created out of thin air, is now something that is superimposed over naked and simple reality, and you know what we do with that right? Let go of, surrender, no longer identify with, laugh at its unreality, and return to the baseline of the No Self Atmosphere, and the simplicity of it.

Emma: Hey Dom, yeah makes sense. I actually still want to cry about losing this identity, so if it comes up again, I'm just going to let it out like before. The anxiety seems to have passed and I had this deep sigh of relief that felt good, just sort of going with all of this no matter how it's all going to turn out is fine. I had a question about enjoying and loving the no self atmosphere. Isn't that also adding something to the atmosphere, which isn't already there?

Dom: Good question. Yes, it is a superimposition and something that has been added to the no self atmosphere. However, it's simply done because those primary facets of the atmosphere already feel good. When there is a state of surrender, openness, effortlessness, complete letting go, no identification, ease, no physical tension, comfort, and so on, it is an aspect of Being, and Being is enjoyable. To Be already IS, and that's why the ego creates all these stories around Being and Isness, because it believes these things to be itself, but Being and Isness exist and are there regardless of whether or not the ego and the 'I'-Thought are attaching to them. Being and Isness are not limited to 'you', they are in fact unlimited aspects of a United reality that will eventually manifest in the No Self Atmosphere.

By introducing at least, a little bit of enjoyment to the no self atmosphere, then there's really no room for the ego to create excuses around spending time in that atmosphere as the baseline of reality. I say this, because I guarantee the ego will make excuses, and I'm sure in your case already has, in order to avoid no longer identifying with it, and resting as the No Self Atmosphere. I went through this for a year, avoiding all of this, and a lot of people who contact me with regards to this process, don't stick around, they just window shop. The fact there are still replies coming from you is pretty big, but the odds are already against you, because most don't follow through with this.

Hence the teaching of Christ: Matthew 7:13 "Enter through the narrow gate. For wide is the gate and broad is the road that leads to destruction, and many enter through it. [14] But small is the gate and narrow the road that leads to life, and only a few find it."

So for experiential Union to manifest, it's something that very few will enter into. So the reason to enjoy this process is so that there starts to be a heartfelt pull to continue with this process or else there is this inundation with fear, crying, and anxiety of the unknown, the feeling of ego death, and many others. Now if this is enjoyed, then all those things that arise, since they are not "enjoyment or baseline" then they can be disidentified from and let go of so there is always this return that happens into the baseline of No Self Atmosphere and the enjoyment of that as being the door into Union, which manifests on its own and in its own time, however long that is to be.

So it's the enjoyment of perceiving that the eyes are seeing all on their own, there is no you seeing, it's a process that happens all by itself, and there is no need to label the nakedness of everything that appears within the stream of sight. Enjoyment of that is happening, but there is no enjoyer!

The enjoyment of perceiving that the ears are hearing all on their own, there is no you hearing, it's a process that happens all by itself, and there is no need to label the nakedness of everything that appears within the stream of hearing.

Then apply the same to the rest: smelling, breathing, touch, feeling, the body, thoughts, awareness, and then when everything has been scanned in this way, and it's found that there is no "you" in any of that, and even the enjoyment of this has no enjoyer, then there is a settling into whatever this moment is like, a surrender into it, a letting go into it, allowing, being with everything as it IS, and cultivating this Atmosphere of No Self as the door to Union, which eventually opens on its own.

Emma: Hey Dom, yeah it all makes sense. So I just had another session in the atmosphere, and the thoughts are just so chaotic and nonstop about all sorts of crazy things. A lot of it is like you mentioned about the past, and random memories were popping up like playing with my favorite dolls and drawing on the sidewalk with chalk. Also there were a lot of thoughts about trying to figure out this whole no self puzzle and how to get Union. And then there were just random thoughts that didn't make sense, it almost seemed like if it was a bunch of TV channels that I was flipping through but sometimes they were all going on at the same time, not sure if that make sense.

I thought the session was going to be wasted, and there was some anger and anxiety about it, but I remembered how you said to allow and I started seeing that whatever the ego was doing, none of it is me, not to identify, and just keep letting go of all of the chaos. So I sort of stayed with that for a while and things did settle down. I had to rescan everything quite a few times to make sure there was no 'me' in the seeing, hearing, breathing, etc, and just returning to the present moment with the thoughts, and then something shifted and I just sat with this shift as long as possible. When it all ended I wrote some descriptions of it in case I forgot.

Everything got real quiet and very simple, almost too simple. The thoughts all became really calm. I mean there were a few thoughts and feelings left like I wanted to start rescanning again, and asking myself if there is a "me" left anywhere in any of the senses or body, and then just sort of settling with whatever was. When everything got real simple even the ego was surprised and making comments about it. I remember many of the remarks were just saying there's no way this is possible. How can this even be real? I'm tricking myself? I guess there was even a wanting to get out of it because it almost seemed surreal. Like there really wasn't anything to do, but just to be with that simplicity of the present moment, and that was fine and it did sort of feel good on its own. But it was surprisingly too much silence and simplicity. Everything was there, the seeing, breathing, body, awareness all there but it all just became I guess I can say closer to being naked just like you described. It was hyper awareness! I was also more in tune with the rest of the body, and with feeling, and just whatever was there is actually a lot of things all at the same time. It's all so rich but all so simple, I can't really explain it, but I don't think this was Union was it?

Dom: That moment of simplicity, as you described it, is the birth of the atmosphere making its way into direct experience. It's starting to manifest aspects of its nature, simplicity and silence are just two factors of many more, and these things will continue to flourish simply by seeing that there is no 'you' in anything.

As far as the chaos of thoughts the ego is creating, that's just a tactic it uses to try to get you to identify with all of it and to continue this unconscious egotistical lifestyle that revolves around the selfishness of the thought 'I', something that is clearly just a thought, an illusion, and day dream. Remember the example of the ego being a spoiled toddler? It's just using all these tactics to say, "Look at me over here, pay me attention, spend time with me or else I will make you remember the past and start conceptualizing the future, LOOK AT ME COME ON!" And what you are doing is just allowing that toddler to say what she wants but without giving her attention so she eventually gets tired and goes to sleep, falls away, disappears. There can be many more moments of the chaotic thought streams that come and go, and remember no matter what comes and goes in the atmosphere of no self, it will always come down to these two choices:

1. Identify with
2. Not Identify with

So with the chaotic thought stream, there was a lot of #1 going on, but eventually you chose #2 and no longer identified with it. When #2 is chosen, then what happens is that whatever is there is no longer identified with, its let go of, surrendered, and allowed to do whatever it does until it eventually falls away, like it did in your experience.

Same thing with anxiety, if it ever comes back again, it will come down to two choices:

1. Identify with
2. Not Identify with

So the No Self Atmosphere, to simplify, is just a constant #2, a constant non-identification with anything and everything plus simple surrender.

In terms of the random memories from childhood, a lot of this is subconscious stuff rising to the surface. The No Self Atmosphere, is a baseline where there is allowance for all the stuff that's just sitting there in the subconscious, things that are perhaps traumas, or unresolved issues, or memories when initial identification with thoughts and body first began to occur, all for the sake of purifying by allowing it to come up, disengaging from it, not identifying with, just allowing it to be there until it falls away on its own and there is a return to baseline.

So this is good, this moment of clarity that was born within the baseline is something that eventually becomes permanent and starts to enter into more and more moments of the day. This is ultimately the next stage with all this work is to see that the baseline of the No Self Atmosphere is always there, all day long, already inherently present, and to begin to tune into and be that atmosphere through every single opportunity and/or micro event of the day.

What I want you to do now is to go back to another lengthier session, say an hour, and also when you do the A.M. practice of establishing the baseline, see if that baseline can be carried into the bathroom. Because the next micro event that happens after the body wakes up in the morning and there's a 20 minute session of establishing the baseline, is that there will be the actual act of physically getting up from bed and walking over to the bathroom in order to urinate, wash hands, brush teeth.

Also any breaks at work, 15 minute breaks, lunch breaks, the drive there and back, trips to the grocery store, any sort of opening in the day that is looser and has less requirements for focusing and thinking, are openings that should be taken advantage of establishing the baseline.

So let's say you have a 15 minute work break and choose to sit in some solitude for a bit in the cafeteria, outside on a bench if it's warm enough, lounge, wherever. So you check again to see, how exactly is direct experience of reality/life taking place? And then start the scan through the senses while establishing that it's all going on all by itself with no you, and eventually coming to rest in the no self atmosphere. When that session is finished, then there should be an attempt to bring that atmosphere into the next experience/micro event of reality. I know I keep reiterating all this stuff, but it's on purpose to make sure it is solidified in your being. Let me know if there are any questions and report back if anything else pops up or details from the next longer session.

Emma: Hey Dom, can you explain how the baseline is always there? I don't have too many other questions besides this one, because it feels like I'm on to something when I read that part of your reply. Thanks.

Dom: Okay, so here's the thing, and you can see this for yourself whether or not this is true. Experience itself, experience of reality, and of life is always happening at every moment that is conscious. There's never a moment when experience isn't happening except during deep sleep, but even in deep sleep, Beingness, or Sleeping is happening, but there's no one there who it's happening to, and there is no consciousness that is even conscious of that experience anyway unless we consider dream states and certain mystical experiences that can happen later.

But we will focus on the 2/3rds of the day when there is conscious awareness and sleep isn't happening. So look and see for yourself. Is there ever a moment throughout the waking day, where there isn't direct experience of reality happening?

Emma: Experience is always happening all day long.

Dom: Okay good, so that experience that's happening, you know that it's there, it's self evident and every moment is an opportunity to check in and see "how is this experience currently experiencing itself?" And with that the question come the two possibilities:

1. Identify with the experience, or aspects of it; thoughts, senses, body, etc.
2. Don't identify with the experience. (Seeing that experience is happening all on its own)

So we are choosing to pick #2 consistently every time so that an experience of life is occurring, but there is no experiencer. So what is experience?

Well, that's when we go into scanning all the senses and making sure #2 is chosen with each one, feeling the body + #2 = seeing that the body is occurring all on its own and there is no bodier. Being aware of thoughts + #2 = seeing that thoughts are occurring but because of #2 there is no thinker, they are all just occurring on their own, and eventually seeing that even perception itself is perceiving all on its own with no perceiver. Perceptions + #2 = perception happening all on its own with no perceiver.

All day long, in every micro event, in every moment, it is always a moment that welcomes the opportunity to ask about direct experience of life, choose not to identify with it personally, start the scan, and eventually settle in a free floating and simply open Atmosphere of No Self as the baseline of experience, and here we return back to the original point: that baseline is ALWAYS there. It's simply a matter of the habitual tendencies of the illusions that the ego creates, which have positioned themselves subconsciously into the senses, experience, the body, and perception, and that's the reason the scan happens so that everything is seen as it is, in the naked format of no longer having any of these identities going.

Understood? We're beyond keeping things simple now, but it's quite necessary to explain it in this way so it gets the intellect pumping, and logic starts wrestling, and reason starts questioning, and intuition starts feeling, and experience starts to adapt to the experiencing of having no experiencer.

Let me know if you need simplification, or rather yet, let me know if you have any other questions and see if you can reiterate what I wrote in this response in your own words.

Emma: Hey Dom, yeah it makes complete sense. Now I get the whole exchange with Adam and taking the A.M. practice into the rest of the day.

What I'm basically doing is falling back into the no self atmosphere of reality, or closest 'door' to Union, and maintaining, actually I can't even really say 'maintain' because that implies there is a me who's doing it, doership, needing to maintain something. Have to find a better way to put it. The atmosphere of no self is what's left over when everything has been let go of, so it's more so a continuous allowing of a sort of non-resistance to everything when all identification has been surrendered and seen though. Right?

Then allowing that to go into more and more of daily experience, and if it isn't that way, then using whatever opportunity I get to allow it to end up that way. Is that it?

Dom: Yeah, that's great. I think you've simplified it better than me. If you go on my YouTube channel, I have all of this explained as video meditations and you can download them as mp3's to listen to them whenever, because sometimes people need to hear it vocally for it all to click and makes sense, just look for the A.M., P.M., and No Self Atmosphere meditations. But it's basically everything that I've describing to you in these e-mails, same exact thing.

https://www.youtube.com/user/snbeings/videos

Emma: Hey Dom, just wanted to let you know I went on your channel and listened to the meditations and downloaded them. It's definitely starting to click, but there's still fear there, like a sense of anxiety of fully letting go into this whole thing. I know you mention dealing with fear by letting it be there, giving it space, and no identifying with it so it falls away, but the fear is just so strong. I had a few incidences of crying and just allowing myself to feel what it's like to be with myself in silence to face all of this without all the distractions. It really sucks to realize I've been running away from myself, from this present moment, by constantly needing to do things, the facebook dramas, wasting time watching pointless shows, and all the ways we try to fill the void. And now facing that void that seems to be what's there when I allow the no self atmosphere to open up, it's just so scary to face what I've been running away from and yet I find that this whole process strangely exhilarating, like intuitively I'm supposed to face my own undoing and this is what will fill the void.

As the day came to end, I did the P.M. practice last night and had the craziest dream, so vivid and colorful. I was going back to my childhood home in the suburbs but there was a tall man there at the door, dressed like some Roman Centurion with his armor and a sword. He wouldn't look at me and stood firmly at the doorway as if he was protecting the way in. I never said anything to him and was a bit scared of what to say, so I walked away. I think the dream is reflecting the fear of letting go, of returning home and the best part was that when I woke up, I was deeply established in that no self atmosphere. The mind came up and started making remarks about the dream, but I was watching the remarks and almost automatically just allowing them to fall away. Everything was very lucid and vivid and my usual morning sluggishness was absent because that hyper awareness was back! So I just laid there like for the A.M. practice. It was still dark out and I just knew I was up before the alarm for the practice, but completely let go of the need to look at the clock because everything was just effortlessly simple and lucid, but at the same time, it was ALL SO DIFFERENT!

That's when I took a deep sigh, I remember you writing about somewhere, or maybe it was in your YouTube vid, I just sort of sighed and let go deeply into whatever and it happened! Everything was One! OMG! I couldn't believe it happened and I got so excited about it and ended up snapping out of Oneness! Shit! Lol! That got the ego going again about how to return to it and a whole storyline of needing to write you and tell you and all these trains of thoughts one after another. Not sure what else to say for now, I'm still a bit overwhelmed by all of this, but it did happen. Thank you so much for everything, I just can't thank you enough!

Dom: Hey Emma, really cool e-mail and so happy for you that grace has opened things up so that at least a glimpse of Union has occurred. What was experienced was the fruit of the No Self Atmosphere starting to mature, however it is yet to be ripened. All you have to do is let go now of any story lines about this, about; " 'I' experienced a glimpse and how do 'I' get it back and what do 'I' do to return to Union?" All of that has to be non-identified with so it too, falls away. That glimpse is what is at the bottom of the No Self atmosphere, it's something that happens on its own when conditions are right, when there is non-identification, surrender, a looseness, no expectations, allowing, flowing, simplicity, zero expectations, zero seeking, rest, etc. So I can say, "Hey cool, 'you' got a glimpse," but no, that's not going to happen. Instead an opening into and experiencing of Oneness happened, but it happened to no One and it comes and goes as it pleases.

So now a return to cultivating No Self Atmosphere, non-abidance, non-identification, A.M./P.M. meditations, and continuing on in this manner.

As far as the dreams, they come and go, and sometimes they provide insight and Union can manifest in a dream so that when the body wakes up, Union is present. This may have happened in your situation where the conditions became just right, however it's nothing to look for or establish more identities around. Whether or not another dream like this happens should be of no concern, non-clinging, non-grasping, simply flowing with the Now where there is no you and it's just a continuous #2, a non-identification of everything.

Let me ask you now at least, after having this experience is there anything to fear with this?

Emma: Hey Dom, God you're so right with all of this. My ego came back with a vengeance trying to figure this all out and playing more games on how to get back to Oneness. It's such a sneaky S.O.B. if you're not aware of what it's doing and end up getting pulled into the storylines and I got suckered into it, or rather there was identifying with 'I' and thoughts.

I get what you're saying with the rest of the e-mail. It's no nonsense and straight to the point. I get it. Don't play ego games, don't label, just return to No Self and it does its own thing! Got it! Much Love, and thanks for everything. I'll check back in with any updates.

Dom: That last paragraph is a gem. In this whole thing, the trickiest part for most people is seeing that this ego isn't who you are, it isn't real, letting it go and surrendering it, etc. It's just a simple seeing of its content, and not identifying with any of it. Just letting it do what it does so it's flowing but without believing that the stream of thoughts is who you are, and this requires consistent seeing and consistent non-identification.

The coolest part is that the ego isn't even real! Who the ego thinks it is, isn't even real at all! This can all be done and over with just like that, a snap of the fingers, just seeing that the ego is an illusion, a daydream with no inherent reality: everything then remains the same, there's still a body that needs food, showering, work, etc. There are still the senses, thoughts still come and go, but the belief that it's happening to anyone is completely seen through when it's seen to be an illusion.

It's a habitual process that started from the day the body (which also isn't who you are) was born. Mom & Dad started using all these labels(words), calling that body 'Emma' and calling other things by other labels/words like "toys, cat, dog, cookie," etc. But none of these things themselves are the same as the labels or words used for them. They are each their own inherent beingness that is united with all beingness.

We are no longer defining anything so everything can be as it is, United, One present experience non-conceptualized, flowing like water, free flowing, allowing and surrendering into all of this when there are no reference points to cling to. Capiche? You don't have write back right away Emma, just let this last e-mail sink in while continuing to fall into the No Self Atmosphere.

Note* All it took was a week later for Emma to write back with an update.

Emma: Hey Dom, it happened again, a bunch of times actually, just like you said when least expected. There was one time in bed on the verge of falling asleep and it was just so amazing, just pure awe, and the ego couldn't help but make comments so it went away again, but there was no worrying about it this time and instead just a return to non identifying and letting go and next thing you know, Oneness again! Yay! It's really interesting how this works because it's the opposite, like getting something only when you don't want it anymore, only it's that everything becomes One thing when there is no you to believe in or hold onto anymore. It's also sort of like a combination lock where you have to turn the lock just right and precisely to the 3 numbers for it to unlock, except instead of three numbers I guess I can call it seeing that the ego isn't me, seeing that everything is occurring all on its own, and being surrendered seems to be it.

It has occurred so many times I've lost track and I wish you can see the smile on my face just thinking about it, ♡♡♡♡. I guess the only question is if Oneness becomes permanent and for longer periods of time if I'm not mistaken from the other exchanges right? Just wanted to let you know how grateful I am for all this and sending lots of Love.

Dom: So great to hear all of this. Yes Oneness eventually becomes permanent because it already is permanent, it's always there like if you step outside of your house, the sky is always there. You just have to check and see, what is that is obstructing or obscuring Oneness from always being the case? Usually it's some sort of identification that's going on, or a rigidity of being in terms of physical tension, stress, lacking surrender, being too much in the headspace and identified with egotism, or the body is being identified with, or any of the senses, or whatever situation is presently unfolding, or for many people it can be fear of full immersion into Oneness and/or wanting or desiring a return to Union. So it's a continuous making sure of there being no identifying with anything at all, and allowing a surrender and acceptance into whatever is left over in that present moment experience that is miraculously happening with no experiencer. Those 3 aspects of the combination lock are brilliant, you summed it up and simplified it perfectly!

From here on out it simply becomes a life of stabilizing Oneness so it's always there, or it is reality for longer and longer periods of time until it's the only reality, and everything else is simply an extension of Oneness, like waves appearing out of the Ocean yet being a part of the Ocean.

You can also look at it from the point of view of the senses. Hearing is always happening, seeing is always happening, breathing is always happening, but usually there is no awareness of these senses occurring because awareness was imprisoned or tied up with the illusions of egotism. When attention is directed to any of the senses, there is usually the thoughts/illusions that are identifying with each sense as in 'I am hearing, I am seeing, I am breathing." Instead, there is a choice of being aware of each sense without identifying with any of them, and this is how the door to Union works. It's simply making sure there is nothing being identified with, so that Union is experienced because it's always there, and it's tuned into by not tuning into anything, non-abidance, non-attachment, non-identification plus a loose surrender.

Also, I can tell you this, with the dozens of people I've worked with in this way whether via e-mail, retreats, the videos, etc, all that needs to be done is the continuous undoing of all identity so that the No Self Atmosphere is always present, always transforming into Oneness. That includes non-clinging to any experiences, non-attachment to Oneness, no identifying with anything that happens, any experiences, any states of consciousness. Got it? Rescan everything and tell me if there is stuckness or identification happening anywhere.

Emma: Hey Dom, yeah everything makes complete sense. There are plenty moments of stuckness and identification to work through. I see it now when typing this reply, or a big one is when talking to others, being in a conversation just seems impossible not to be identified and ego'ed into the whole thing. I think it can be done in time though by being aware and just kind of surrendered when talking. I'll have to experiment with it like you said.

Oneness manifests mostly in relaxed moments like on the sofa when relaxing or watching a movie, driving, when going to sleep, but never really happens in any of the active periods you described in your video. The whole exchange with Adam is just so great to read though, and it really breaks this all down perfectly.

Can you comment on the no self atmosphere during active moments? These are mostly the times when I get caught up in the illusions or identifying with a 'me'.

Dom: Hey Emma, you can start by putting on your favorite music, playlist, album, whatever it is, just dance to it. Let the body do whatever it wants to the music and allow the No Self Atmosphere to be established while movement is happening. The only difference this time around is that when scanning of the body and senses is happening so that any identification is seen through and surrendered, it's done so while this movement is happening. Eventually when getting to the movement of the body itself, it's the same as everything else; dancing is happening and there is no dancer. Feeling the music is happening but there is no feeler. Keeping the rhythm is happening, but there is no keeper of the rhythm. That whole dance, that whole movement in the present moment of the body is all happening by itself and doesn't require a belief in any 'you' for it to happen. Got it?

Same deal when going for walks. When I do retreats twice a year, I'll go on walks and explain how to deconstruct walking in this same manner as dancing. It's practically the same thing; walking is happening all on its own and there is no walker, each step one before the other all going on, on its own, without a 'you'. In this same manner, moving on to all the other senses because they become so involved in a walk; the wind hitting the skin, the sun, the temperature, all the smells and all the sights. It's a big deal to deconstruct this whole thing when walking, but the root in all of it is that it's an experience that's happening without an experiencer.

Conscious experience is there first, and then it's just a matter of allowing experience to be free flowing without an experiencer, without any identification in any senses, and the biggest one of all is detaching and not identifying with the story lines of illusion that the mind is creating and presenting, and then everything becomes effortless.

So applying the No Self Atmosphere to various activities is how to further deepen and integrate all of this. Got it?

Emma: Hey Dom, yeah got it! This is all so crazy cool I got just goose bumps from this reply. So I read it twice, but the first time there was plenty of identification going on and stuckness. Maybe it's like subtle identification going on just out of habit. I can't seem to pinpoint where or what it is, but it seems bodily and out of habit. When I reread your reply the second time around I did it in the way you described in the reply, just surrendered and aware that reading is happening without a reader, and even understanding the teachings is happening on its own, and just being very surrendered and flowing with the reading and it just really makes sense now. It's like I'm bringing, or rather, allowing the no-self atmosphere to come into actions. So neat and makes perfect sense! I'll try the dancing thing out too for sure and report back with any updates. Thanks so much again, life will never be the same again, lol!

Note* A few weeks pass by until getting another reply from Emma. Usually at this point, anything I say becomes repetitive in a reply, but it acts as a reminder to reiterate these same points so that they go beyond being just intellectually understood, and become actual experiential insights. For Emma, it all just really clicked and flowed.

Emma: Hey Dom, you were right again about establishing all of this into activities. Oneness is now making appearances in the most unforeseen circumstances it's all just so amazing, I don't even have words for any of this and just want to cry from joy!

The dancing practice is phenomenal and is just great to work through any identification, it's just cathartic and beautiful but I find I lose myself in the dance but in more of an unconscious fashion and not necessarily into Union. So I started tweaking the dance and trying to be present and aware while also not identifying and seeing everything as happening without me in it and that really helped a lot and made sense, and applying the same with the walks. After a few weeks of applying this, Oneness just started happening off and on throughout the day and it's always so exhilarating, kind of takes your breath away at the magnitude of the experience.

Yesterday I had the day off and some time to sit in meditation and it happened again, but this time it was just so deeply established. I was able to shift positions when the legs lost circulation and even got up to use the bathroom all while everything was One united experience. It's just the biggest trip and yet feels perfect, everything just as it should be, crystal clear and One with no me in it anywhere, WOW!

Eventually I had to attend to some bills and online stuff and Oneness disappeared when using the discriminating mind, but it all makes sense now and I do feel like it's always there in the background, just waiting to become fully present for me to disappear into. Just wanted to say it's definitely becoming more and more of my, or rather, of reality and experience itself. At various times, even thinking can occur while Union is present.

Anyway, I have to run off, or rather running off to the things of life is happening with no me in any of it, lol ;)

Note* All that's left, to reiterate, is a continuation of establishing and being rooted into this No Self Atmosphere of non-identification with the Ego, Senses, Body, Perception, Awareness and this will allow all the true nature of reality to manifest all on its own for deeper and longer periods of time, until one day waking up happens all on its own as Oneness.

***

CHAPTER 5

CHRISTINA'S EXCHANGE

With Christina there was a lot of work on two different levels. The first was that before we could even get to the process of direct Seeing/Perceiving what happens in her reality, and starting to deconstruct things, there was a ton of psychological fragmentation around the different belief systems that were fed into her from an institutionalized Western version of Christianity. Instead of something that was meant to be a living and breathing mystical ego death which leads to Spiritual rebirth, Love, acceptance, and finally Union, it instead worked up in Christina a number of mental loops that included things like, "I will never be worthy, self hatred for being a sinner, never being good enough for God, lots of guilt, and the list of constructs goes on and on.

It took a while to work through these things with her, including coming from a nonjudgmental and empathic place of listening and explaining that she is loved and that God is waiting for her to get out of the way so that Union can take place (like the Westerners say, let go and Let God). We didn't initially resolve all of the fragmentations because I knew it could literally take years of counseling and healing to resolve all of this, when really all that needed to be resolved is to see that the root of all of this drama is the false identity of the 'I-Thought.' Eventually when enough trust was gained, she decided to give the process a go, but the next hang up was mostly on the level of having an intellectual understanding of what was being said, but not having the ability to perceive this for herself. Eventually, this hang up would resolve and lead to quite the realizations.

The following exchange took place after I had already sent her some pdf exchanges that I had completed successfully with other people, to various degrees of course, and shows the moment when the intellectual hang up is resolved. (From here on I refer to Christina as Chris, as she herself preferred.)

Chris: Okay, so I did like you said and read the notes you have with the other people, and reread them several times just trying to do like you said, feel it, intuit it, and play with it, and I'm still here, still the same, and nothing has changed. It has only been a few days though, and I mostly forget to see for myself and play with the different perspectives, but I have set aside some time during lunch breaks and driving like you suggested. The thing is, I understand what you're saying, but I don't really know if I feel it.

Dom: Okay, I will explain this in a different way, however, promise me you'll reread what I'm about to say at least once a day until it really sticks, just like you have with what I sent you already, okay?

When a baby is born, it is simply aware and that's it, just alive and aware, and nothing else.

So what starts to happen? The parents, or single parent, start to use these things called words around the baby, while they point to things. So the mother will point to herself and say, "Mommy," or point to the Father and say, "Daddy," and so forth. Then, every time the parents are around this Baby, they start using a name around it, say for example Daisy.

Now initially, this baby is just aware and alive and that awareness is taking everything in, all at once, without any concepts, or constructs, or names, or labels. The baby doesn't care if anything has a name or not because everything is just happening as it's happening, just arising on its own, and this baby is watching and taking everything in without thoughts, or ideas, or labels, or any of the things the parents are using.

Remember what Christ said, Matthew 18:3 "Verily I say unto you, Except ye be converted and become like children, ye shall not enter into the kingdom of heaven."

So there is the first level of all of this. The newborn Child is crystal clear, alive, awake, pure, watching, taking in, and there are no ideas, words, concepts, names, or anything there except directly Seeing and taking in all that is occurring.

So the process I'm describing is a sort of 'Seeing' directly all these initial things picked up by parents, then later the additional baggage that came from peers, television, school, society, world, hurts/pains, fragmentations, and even various troubles that arose in the mind because of religion, so that you revert to this Childlike freedom and awareness of just Seeing everything nakedly, and surrendering to whatever happens.

The root of all the problems is when the baby learns the word 'I' and then starts to detach from the openness of everything that's going on, and instead attaches to this imaginary word ('I') it was taught. Whereas before when the baby was hungry, it would lead to crying, all happening on its own and spontaneously. When the baby was tired, falling asleep would happen all on its own. But now with this newly imagined thought, 'I', this same openness and spontaneous happening of all things on their own, is now starting to be labeled with this imagined 'I'.

So now in the baby's mind, it is starting to correlate the feeling of an empty stomach with the imagination that "I am hungry, I want food, I want mommy, I am sleepy, I want cookies, I want toys," and the root of illusion takes hold.

So one more time Chris, again, I'm reminding you to re-read this until it really sinks in okay?

Chris: Yes I will reread like the other stuff and I think I understand what you're saying. Since I've been reading some of the exchanges, I've had a few experiences while driving where there weren't hardly any thoughts going on in my brain at all, it was just quiet and it even surprised me a bit because I wasn't used to it. Not sure what that was but you did say that some insights might start to happen and maybe that was one? So is not having any thoughts sort of like being that baby?

Dom: In those moments there is no 'I-thought' active, or in your case no thoughts at all, and yet everything was still happening right? There was still an ability to drive, focus on the road, pay attention, and get to the right destination yes?

Chris: Yes all of that stuff still happened.

Dom: See, so that is direct proof and direct experience that this "I-Thought" isn't necessary to be able to function normally in life. Everything still happened as it was supposed to and yes that was a little bit of grace revealing stillness and peace.

However, what I really want to focus on is this moment where there was a 'Seeing/Perceiving' that there were no thoughts occurring. Do you remember clearly what that was like, what it felt like, details, specifics?

Chris: I guess I'm just so used to the nonstop thoughts, that I noticed the brief periods of no thought. They were short though, the first one maybe 10 seconds. But then again the next day during both drives that moment came back again and there was lots of peace there.

But then my mind, that 'I' made a comment about it, something like, "Oh this is cool and new, how is this even possible?" And of course that let the flood of thoughts back in. So is this the goal, to get into no thoughts?

Dom: First you are already starting to see the mind, or the 'I-Thought,' in a third person narrative, or external, just by the comments. So can you keep this going? Every time the mind is thinking, or the 'I-Thought' pops up, to see it as not you, as something external, as something that isn't even real? Just like how you noticed the thoughtless moments, can you make it a habit to notice everything the mind thinks, every time the mind thinks, and see that it isn't who you are?

Second, the goal isn't to reach thoughtlessness, because that implies there is an 'I' seeking some goal. In the people who unravel Union, sometimes there is thoughtlessness and sometimes not, but that has no effect on Union. The point is to no longer identify with thoughts, to see that they are all imaginary and unreal constructs, illusions that play out right before awareness.

Chris: I get what you're saying, but that seems so hard.

Dom: Just like any habit, it takes some time and practice before it becomes second nature, and this is a habit that can lead to Union, so I would definitely call that something very valuable. How about this, I'm going to

116

finish this sentence with an insult, just for the purpose of you being able to see what the 'I-Thought' does okay? Here it is: I don't like Christina and I wish she would just directly see what I'm saying here, or else we're both wasting precious time."

Now can you tell me immediately what reactions do you see/feel from that insult?

Chris: I don't like it. I'm confused and feel a bit hurt why you would even say that, and a bit angry.

Dom: That's it right there! You just directly saw what the ego is doing, look all the times 'I' is referenced in that sentence. First comes the thought 'I' followed by all the other things; don't like, confusion, hurt, angry.

Now I want you to do two things. The first is, since you know that the insult was false and just used to show an example, do you agree that all those feelings, reactions, thoughts, and responses are no longer necessary?

Chris: Yeah, I get what you're saying. It was just an initial reaction to the insult.

Dom: So the second thing is can you now let go of all of them? See that they are all unnecessary and let go, surrender all of them. You can do so with a deep breath, a deep exhale, a sigh, maybe loosen any tightness in the body, in the stomach, in the spine, check and see if there is any tightness in the body anywhere that arose along with those reactions, and if you find them, loosen them as part of the surrender and letting go of all of those reactions, can you do that and get back to me with some notes after its successful?

Chris: Yes I'm doing so now and I will get back to you.

Dom: When you do reply, can you do it without referring to yourself as 'I'? So instead of "I felt like this and that," try replying without using the word 'I' at all, so similar to; "It felt like this and that, or a feeling occurred, etc."

Chris: Okay so this took a while to respond to and had to be erased and rewritten several times because of the I-word. It felt like there was tightness and tension in the whole body because of the reaction, and there was an ability to notice and let go of all these things like you mentioned, but it took a while to do so.

Dom: So let's try it again, only this time, notice the reactions, but don't attach the 'I-Thought" to the reactions. Here we go: No one in their life has ever liked Christina, they only pretended to.

Now, allow the 'Seeing/Perceiving' to notice the reactions, but without attaching anything to them, without attaching 'I', or 'Me', or any identities at all and tell me what is it like.

Chris: Wow, yeah that's extremely interesting. I mean this time the reactions weren't as bad as before because I know the insult trick better now, and I'm more aware, but it's interesting to watch the reactions take place while trying to not attach to them. I can see how it's hurt that's arising, and some anger, surprise, but I don't have to claim them or attach to them, is that right?

Dom: Exactly. Anytime any emotions, reaction, feeling, or thought arises, if there is enough 'Seeing/Perceiving' established as a habit, then it makes it much more easier to start letting go of all these things and no longer identifying with them. If you keep doing that, then everything will fall away eventually and reveal Union.

So do you see now what I mean about forming this habit of seeing the reactions, feelings, and thoughts that surround this "I-Thought"? And not just from my example insults, but from every single daily life experience, someone calls your name, someone cuts you off in traffic, you read something posted on facebook by an old friend, your parents give you advice, your sister wants to borrow money, a child smiles at you, a scary movie, and so on, all these things are making this 'I-Thought' react in all these different ways, adding feelings, adding different emotions, and you are believing this false daydream to be you.

So create this habit of seeing it, and letting it go, seeing that it isn't even real.

Note* At this point I hadn't heard from Chris for over a month, which was usually the case with a number of people I was corresponding with via e-mail, phone, Skype. Eventually she came back to reply with some insights and experiences. The grace was beginning to manifest as different experiences and as usual, it does so differently in different people. For Chris, there were various moments that broke up how she was used to experiencing reality, and eventually it all culminated in an explosion of light.

Chris: Yeah, I've been doing this and it feels like I'm more self conscious of this thinking process and a lot of times when the thought 'I' pops up, but more times than not, I forget, or I'll catch it after the fact. It's such a sneaky bastard, like a bad habit that you can't kick. There's definitely something different going on. I've had some very lucid dreams and I'm having more periods of thoughtlessness, but the mind keeps coming back to comment on these moments, except that the thing with the surrender has been helping. So if there is no thought and the mind comes back to comment on it, I just let go of the comments and return right back to thoughtlessness and kind of this loose surrender you've described in the exchanges. The other thing is I've had some very surreal moments, I guess I can say super aware of everything, sort of like lucid dreaming except entirely awake. They were very short but VERY amazing experiences and I'm seriously excited about all of this.

Dom: I want to ask you, in these lucid experiences, did the mind come in and start trying to figure out what was going on?

Chris: Yeah, I know what you're going to say. The mind makes it disappear just like the thoughtless moments. It's exactly what I did, or rather what happened with the mind's reaction, but there was such overwhelming excitement and awe, and then wondering how this is even happening and if other people could tell.

Dom: Yes, exactly what I was going to say. You're starting to intuit the teachings, which is good, and you're right, next time any experiences happen, just keep surrendering to them, keep letting go of the minds reactions or needs to want to analyze or understand the experience, because as in life, the best experiences are ones where the mind has gotten out of the way of the experience, so there is just that naked childlike wonder, awe, and awareness taking it all in, understood? It's really simple, it's just seeing that the mind is all daydreams, illusions, imaginations, and a continuous seeing that none of those things are you. This is actually a relief and surrender becomes real. All those burdens of being someone, having to do something, seeking, wanting, desiring, confusion, the past pains and traumas, all things that belong to a supposed "someone" which is just a fiction, can be let go of and it is a true sigh of relief.

Also it takes time to solidify this Seeing/Perceiving so that it is strengthened and can cut through all of the daydreams. You can even skip all that if you could just see the unreality of this "I-Thought". I want you to do a thought experiment/exercise and just work with this alone for a few days.

I want you to imagine 4 things: A golden halo, a tiny female gnome, a cloud, and the 'I-Thought'. Now you can add whatever details you like to the halo, gnome, and cloud, but leave the 'I-Thought' as it's always been.

So memorize these four things and think about each one in different orders. So something similar to this: Gnome, halo, 'I-Thought" cloud, halo, cloud, gnome, I-Thought, halo, cloud…..and so forth. Spend maybe only two to four seconds on each before switching to the next.

Notice that these first three thoughts (halo, gnome, cloud) aren't real, they are daydreams, illusions, complete fabrications that only exist as make believe, and the I-Thought is also a daydream, illusion, complete fabrication, and only exists as make believe.

You can't even show me the halo, or the gnome, or the cloud, or the 'I-Thought' because 'I' is just made up, a false belief. Seriously spend some time practicing and playing with this and tell me in your direct experience if you see this to be true directly. Is it 'I' who is thinking these thoughts, or are thoughts occurring on their own without an 'I' needed for them to occur? Take your time.

Note* Again, it was several weeks before hearing from Chris again, but when I did hear from her, it was clear she had seen the illusion of the 'I'.

Chris: Yeah wow, this is crazy, yeah I get it, I see it as an experience now how it's just some sort of make believe thing, I mean not only that, but everything we think, isn't even real, they're all just daydreams, the whole thought process is like a stream of nonstop illusions. It's like watching a TV channel that plays nonstop all day going from one scene to the next, then to other topics, which lead to other subjects, all centered around the 'I' just like you said. Wow, it's just so ridiculously selfish, the world revolving only around this false 'I', lol.

There is no difference between those imagined things in the practice and the 'I'. I mean, I tried to justify that there has to be a difference in so many ways, until I noticed that every time I consciously brought up the thought 'I' that it was referencing my body and how it feels and all the things going on it.

But then I was thinking about the whole baby ordeal and Jesus' teaching about returning to being a child again and how the parents start using the 'I' word as a self reference that doesn't even need to be there. So I sort of went back as far as I could to my memories as a little girl, just really going along to see if I remember a moment where this 'I' all started and I remembered a moment in the summer where I was playing with all the other kids in one of those kiddy pools in my cousin's backyard.

I didn't have a care in the world until one of the other girls said she didn't like the color of my swimsuit and that she liked red better than pink, before running off somewhere. And I just looked down at my swimsuit and started questioning its color, and myself, and I became really self conscious that day around the other kids, even asking my mother to change out of the swimsuit, but she refused. So I remained really self conscious and shy, and I just feel like this self conscious thing had some deeper connection to the false 'I' especially after seeing how unreal it is.

Anyway, it all kind of came together for me through surrender and luckily I was lying on my sofa before this all exploded. I let go of that moment I remembered, just surrendered the self consciousness and fully let go of it knowing that the 'I' that attaches to it isn't even real anyway. It was really feeling it all. Feeling this body and feeling the self consciousness, and eventually feeling the surrendering of all of that.

I don't know exactly how this happened, but there was definitely some fear because it just feels like everything was going to fall down, or fall away into something unknown. I thought it was me that was scared at first, but I'm just so sick and tired of everything as it's been so far, all the pains and hurts, and living life from this false identity. It's almost like my trust in God, of letting go of everything false and just having trust in your instructions a well, allowed me to even let go of the fear.

It took a few days because every time there was this thorough surrender of all things, of how I see myself, feel myself, my self image, self conscious, ideas, looks, clinging to what the world thinks the body should look like, everything that can be thought of and felt, would start to bring me to this place of fear of letting go further, like what will happen when everything falls away? But I got used to the fear being there and let go of the fear too.

The final result was like I fell down and into an explosion of light and bliss, it was such an amazing shock and no matter how in awe of everything I was, the light and the bliss were still there and it was almost impossible to handle all that was going through me, or rather all that was happening when there was no longer any me, so there was just even more surrender if that makes sense, to it even more, and in that moment I disappeared into the light, and was the light, but also I was the bliss and it was me, it was so crazy and so powerful more than anything I ever experienced with the Holy Spirit, and I'm writing you right now still from that place as its flowing through me and everywhere all at once. It's like a never ending space that I melted into and I just can't thank you enough and I've cried from gratitude and from Love and it feels like a direct connection to God but I would have never imagined it ever to be like this! Wow! With the Holy Spirit it was very light and gentle and this is the most intense experience I've ever had, is this how it's supposed to be? I don't know where I am anymore because I'm everywhere and can't pinpoint anyplace that's me.

Dom: Listen Chris, I'll write more to you later. Just know that this is all a perfect process and you've accessed the heart and light of God through the central channel, and this is the way Union has started to manifest for you. Like you read in some of the other exchanges, it's very peaceful and still, and the love doesn't come until much later, while for others it can show up all at once. The spark of light is something to delve deeper into and start to live from by accepting and allowing it to grow, along with all the other manifestations that are there, just continue to spend time with all of this as it's a very valuable, important, and precious time, and if that means taking a few days off work to allow this to integrate and stabilize, then don't hesitate.

A continuous letting go and surrendering of all things into whatever remains, whether it is stillness, peace, thoughtlessness, further thoughts/emotions arising to be surrendered, or anything else that manifests, it has to be all seen, surrendered, and let go of until there is a manifestation of Union that is stabilized and rested in.

Chris: I'm just shaking and crying from the beauty and the gratitude is so magnificent and vast that it's too big to try to even put into words. God bless you Dom, I will stay with all of this for a while and get back to you.

Note* I gave her a week before checking back in, as I've found that a seven day period is usually substantial enough to check and see if the more expressively intense realizations were permanent or passing glimpses, and in Chris, there was no end to it.

Dom: Hey Chris, just checking in to see how are things holding up.

Chris: Hey Dom, my God things will never be the same again, the dreams are all lucid and the content has changed. There are angels that were talking to me in them, full color and fully lucid. There is no possible way to contain the love and that's just a tiny percentage of its fullness, so I realized the only way that sort of Love can come through us is if you are out of the way of it, or you see that there is no you to get in the way of it just like you were saying. It's also hard to make out any boundaries, like I don't know where God ends and I begin, or the other way around, I think you know what I'm referring to. My family has noticed something's changed in me, people are talking at work since I finally made it in after taking some days off like you suggested, oh and everyone is AMAZINGLY beautiful and you can see the life that animates each one, even people I (or the judgmental ego) would have before deemed average or unattractive, or whatever judgments would come to the ego, now have this living essence of life that flows through them, through all things, everything is just fascinating to look at, it's all breathing and alive. I just can't thank you enough and also had a couple questions. Will it always be like this and is this the state that Jesus lived from?

Dom: Yeah, it sounds like Union has manifested. This isn't the end by no means, but just the beginning, it is the true birth, being born again into Union and this is nothing compared to how it will all change and evolve further on, and things will settle down as well eventually, so just breath and continue the letting go and surrendering of whatever things arise. So now, certain aspects of Union won't always be like they are currently and only time will tell how it flowers for you. Also, as to Jesus, yes he lived this exact Union and prayed that we may all be One as he and the Father are One in John 17:21. Listen, just spend some time with all of this and let it all stabilize and integrate into daily life, then get back to me in a week or two and let me know how things are holding up.

Note* A few weeks later she checks back in.

Chris: Hi Dom, so yeah you were right, everything has settled down but everything is still so different than before, it's truly a joy unspeakable. I'm noticing there are all sorts of interesting things the mind is showing me and it's almost like it's trying to get me to pay attention to it by showing me visions, new ideas, I've had some experiences of being shown things that would happen a few days later, and some memories from childhood, and a bunch of different emotions arising. A lot of times I sort of get caught up being fascinated by the things being shown within and tend to get wrapped up in them before snapping back to reality. Can you explain what's going on?

Dom: Yes, I can explain, but tell me is there still Oneness with no boundaries?

Chris: It seems to come and go, like I know how to sort of surrender and fall into it, then it's there. But it's not always there and it seems like there's a falling out of it a lot.

Dom: Okay, so what you need to do, is notice what are the things that cause a falling out of Union, and continue to let go and surrender these things continuously so there are no attachments or identifications with them. There has to be a learning to live from the place of Union. Let me ask if you are you able to talk to other people from the place of Union?

Chris: No, I'm not. It's mostly when I'm alone, driving, falling asleep, on lunch break, about to a nap, and so on.

Dom: So you have to be able to again learn to live from the place of Union so it's stabilized and integrated with the rest of life, by noticing all of the details of how it all works and what creates this separation from Union to occur.

Chris: Okay, I think I understand. I think it's when I'm focused more externally to the outer world and what people are saying and what I need to do that makes the Union disappear. Is that right?

Dom: Yes, you are starting to pick up on it. So try being completely surrendered and in this place of falling vertically back into the Union whenever your attention is externalized, and see if you can continue to talk from there, or do anything from there. Considering you can drive while Union is in place, do the same with other things. Try riding your bike in the same way, eating in the same way, brushing teeth in the same way, showering in the same way, going on walks in the same way, eventually talking to people in the same way...I think you see the pattern here.

Chris: Yeah, I do. What about all the mind stuff continuing to show all sorts of incredible things?

Dom: It's just more illusions and subconscious material that is arising for the sake of purification. Whatever arises, just 'Seeing' that it is there, without really buying into its reality, and continuously surrendering and letting go of whatever scenes, memories, emotions, whatever is being produced or arising. Do so from a place of love and acceptance, while surrendering and letting go. Or else your awareness again gets kidnapped by the illusions and further identities such as, " I like what the mind is showing me, I wonder what all this stuff is, how do I deal with this stuff, I think this stuff is really interesting….." and so on. All of that has to be seen as not you, as unreality, surrendered and let go of, even after access to Union develops just for the sake of Union being able to be completely unobstructed by the attachment to mental objects, to emotional feelings, to the body, and to any imagined identities, does this make sense?

Chris: Wow, yeah that makes perfect sense. There are so many past hurts and traumas there, past breakups, emotional turmoil, all the past breakdowns, issues with my parents, other's I've wronged, it's just so much stuff coming up and you're saying to just continue letting go of it all? That seems hard but makes complete sense.

Dom: It's only hard if you believe this imagined thing called "hard" which isn't even real, and you haven't even deeply gone into what I've proposed yet. Every time any of those things arises, if you allow the mind to say, "Wow, this is hard, I don't really want to remember or deal with this," then that's just an additional identification, another daydream, another untrue illusion, and there is a running away from healing and resolving the past. Go do it now: Accepting and open to whatever arises, from a place of love and acceptance, allowing whatever arises to be there for as long as it needs to be without running away from it, without judging it, and just seeing that this thing that has arrived, isn't who you are and can be let go of and surrendered. Get back to me when you do this and tell me how it went. Spend a few days or a week with it and get back and tell me what you find.

Chris: Hi Dom, I'm back and have some interesting things to share. So it took a bit of getting used to what you originally proposed and I really had to feel my way through it, but I think I got the hang of it. I realized that when talking to others, there is more tightness, like being tense, in the stomach, pretty much the whole body. I don't know if it's because I've been used to just being attentive to others and picked it up out of habit or not, but anyhow, I realized this was going and started really working with this, just being physically loose and surrendered like I usually am when I'm by myself, or when Union tends to reappear.

So the other day my Mother stopped by my place unannounced when I was watching a movie with my little ones, and I got so annoyed by her interruption because my youngest daughter had fallen asleep during the movie after being feisty and fidgety all day, but then woke up. So here I am, in the middle of a rage taking over at her audacity to interrupt a peaceful time, and of course we get into an argument and I end up being really mean to her right, but I realized and was seeing all of this all of a sudden take place like I had dropped into Union, like I was the room, and I was my mother, and I was my daughters, and I was being unnecessarily mean to myself instead of my mother. It was the first time the Union experience happened in the midst of talking to someone, and being mean too, lol. So of course, I immediately dropped all the annoyance, and rage and apologized and hugged her, and when my daughter woke up and saw her, ran to her and hugged her all happy anyway, so all was good.

I made her some tea and just did like you said; continuously surrendering a lot of stuff I didn't even realize there was in the ego that only arises around my mother. A lot of judgments, annoyance, resistance to her presence, a desire for her to go away and leave me alone, and SO MUCH MORE! All of it revolving around the false identity of 'I', of course which is false. So you know after all that was let go of, it's like I truly saw her for the first time in my life, just like her raw essence and all the imperfections of her own ego being molded by all the life crap she went through and seeing that behind all that there is this warrior in her, this strong woman who has gone through so much and is still here today, and the way her eyes shined. It was like I saw her as a brand new being and because all the judgments were gone, we could be friends, sisters, and it really felt like there weren't any more of these daughter hang ups to get in the way of us, just really fascinating. Oh and Union stayed throughout the experience and she knew something was up with me, but I told her I'll save it for another day when I can give her some of the exchanges you sent me. Well guess what she said when I mentioned that? She said, "You'd think I wouldn't know about some things, but you'd be surprised how much life teaches when you allow it to." Crazy huh?

Anyway, lots of gratitude and Love and like you said, this just feels like the beginning of a new life and a new birth. Obviously things were never going to be the same again, but in this case, the continuation of this process just keeps revealing beautiful gifts and revelations.

Dom: Chris, yeah that's powerful and very beautiful, and that's just something that happened with your mother, so imagine when it is applied to everyone else, in every experience, at every time of the day so that Union is stabilized and integrated to always be there.

As far as the experience of just being mean to yourself instead of your mother, which happened when all the borders to reality disappeared in Union, take a look at this verse.

Matthew 25:35(NIV) For I was hungry and you gave me something to eat, I was thirsty and you gave me something to drink, I was a stranger and you invited me in, I needed clothes and you clothed me, I was sick and you looked after me, I was in a prison and you came to visit me.

Then the righteous will answer him. 'Lord. When did we see you hungry and feed you, or thirsty and gave you something to drink? When did we see you a stranger and invite you in, or needing clothes and clothe you? When did we see you sick or in prison and visit you?

The King will reply, 'Truly I tell you, whatever you did for one of the least of these brothers and sisters of mine, you did for me.'

You see, you were directly experiencing how your Mother isn't necessarily a separate individual, but One with the Oneness, unified, linked, the Omnipresence of God's Oneness deconstructs the illusions of separation and divisions.

The rest is like I said, a continuation of what I mentioned in this last e-mail so that the last vestiges of the illusions and habitual impurities can be seen through and surrendered/let go of experientially, physically, emotionally, totally, and completely so that Union shines through as the true permanent reality.

Furthermore, don't even identify with Union as being anything that you have, because as you know, there is no 'you' in Union, it is its own Oneness. So even trying to claim that as 'yours', or as an 'I' that is having access to it, and re-wrapping the fiction of an 'I' around it has to also ultimately be surrendered as well. Understood?

Chris: Yes Dom, clear as the sky today here through my window. Union only manifests anyway when the 'I' is seen as a fabrication and surrendered, so I do understand completely what you're saying, since I'm seeing how there can be all these subtle levels to identity that we aren't even aware of. It's all continuing though, like you said. Honestly, this thing is kind of taking on a life of its own. There really isn't much for me to do because everything is happening on its own, life, raising children as a single mother, work, school activities, meditation, and prayer is just spontaneous, it's all one huge flow that continues now since there is no me to get in the way of it and it's fascinating on so many levels.

Even on really busy days with work and kids and cooking, I'm talking 18 hour days were before I just wouldn't be able to do it all, now it's like since there is no me in the way of the day, there is a strength and power found in Union where everything happens so effortlessly and quite amazing with such softness and beauty. Thank you Dom so much for your time and patience, I'm really grateful of all your time and the exchanges were such beautiful gifts, I've started sharing them with some friends and with my mom as well, so don't be surprised if you get a few more e-mails.

Dom: Thank you Chris, all thanks to the One, the Supreme all pervasive Omnipresent One whose will manifests through us when we realize we were in the way of it by believing in the fiction of a make believe identity. No worries on the e-mails, just keep sending them this way and I'll send some more exchanges I'm lining up with a few others who have finally realized Union, so your friends and family can get a better grasp on this. I'll check back in to see how things are flowering in a month or so. Lots of Love!

***

CHAPTER 6

QUESTIONS & ANSWERS

Question: How do I start with everything? I just read a bunch of exchanges and I understand this all intellectually, but how do I go about experiencing all of this?

Answer: Start by letting go of 'I' and letting go of wanting to start anything. Then become aware of the ego, of thoughts and how they are all unreal illusions, unreal labels, unreal concepts, unreal fairy tales and illusion based storylines.

Spend 15 minutes with a pen and a piece of paper and write down the content of the ego and all the things the ego thinks about, all its story lines, and the different directions and train of thoughts it goes down. Got it? Now after that's done, make this a habit that happens all day long, but also add, no longer identifying with anything the ego creates. Just let it be, let continue to spit out its story lines about who it thinks you are, and the body, and emotions, and desires, and seeking, whatever its content just let that content continue but without identifying with any of it, while also seeing that none of the content is real anyway, all illusions, all lies, none of which is who you are, all happening on its own.

Since none of that is you, it's a huge relief, so allow everything to be as it is, a deeply breathed existential sigh into allowing things to be as they are with no you in any of it. It's now okay to just surrender into non-being, into no self, into whatever it is that is left over when nothing is identified with.

To deepen this, do the AM/PM meditations, cultivate the Atmosphere of No Self meditation in every possible daily situation in both passive and active situations, set aside an hour a day to sit in this manner, simplify and minimize television, social media, and all things that create the ego believing and reconstructing an 'I', and this will eventually gain steam, day after day, week after week, until Union manifests on its own when least expected.

It's a constant cultivation of everything being as it is without any identifications with any thoughts, body, people, places, things, emotions, feelings, labels, ideas, physical tensions or tightness, and surrendering/letting go into whatever is left over when there are no reference points to anything, nothing to hold on to, nothing to identify with.

Question: Can you describe what exactly the ego is in a simplified manner? Technically I get it from reading the exchanges, but I just wanted to see if it fits what I think it is. Thanks.

Answer: The ego is just a conglomerate of thoughts and the root of the ego is the thought 'I' which then extends to: 'I, me, mine'. If I ask you the question, who do you think you are, the answers you come up will all be thoughts, labels, ideas, imaginations, and any answer that you give me is another aspect of that ego.

For example anything that you fill in the black here: 'I am _____(fill in the blank).' That 'I' that 'am' and anything that gets filled in that blank is part of the Egoic belief construct. That blank is usually filled in with name, body, gender, belief system, age, race, ethnicity, culture, nationality, job title, personhood, and so forth.

It's also the thought streams that are continuously occurring. Sit down for 5-10 minutes and simply watch, or become conscious of, the streams of thoughts that the mind produces. This stream is being identified with as your stream and your thoughts, and that is also an aspect of the ego.

The Ego is all the thoughts and beliefs in what you take yourself to be, in the belief of this you, in the belief that you are that body and that you are the one having that stream of thoughts and the experience of life, along with all the labels, filters, biases, ideas, constructs about everything.

During deep sleep, there is no ego and when that body you believe to be you was in a newborn state of being, there also was no ego. All of reality is occurring prior to the beliefs that the ego is constructing and reality is not limited to beliefs.

The ego is simply the illusions, daydreams, imaginations, thoughts, concepts, and ideas that filter daily reality and experience.

Question: After reading those exchanges, it boggles my mind how fast all of the people you corresponded with were able to experience Union. Yet here I am, weeks later after reading and re-reading, and I'm still here, still believing in the ego stories. Is this process supposed to happen that fast and do some people just not get this?

Answer: The exchanges you've read are compressed and edited down to the most vital points. In fact, with each of these individuals, the process took anywhere from a few weeks at the soonest to more than 6-12 months in some instances.

It's also a path and lifestyle that stays with you and becomes a permanent aspect of life and it matures over the years, becoming richer, deeper, and fuller as the years go by. Besides deconstructing the ego, the later stages deconstruct reality as well in terms of no longer believing in programmed beliefs/dualities/paradigms such as up vs. down, left vs. right, inside vs. outside, me vs. you, and so forth. These are things that are continuously deconstructed as you go through all the various ups and downs of life's situations, which are rather active and living spiritual exercises where there is a choice to identify with the old status quo programming, or to be fully in Union through it all.

As for some people not getting this, it's true, quite a few people don't get this and the reasons vary as much as people do. Even for me, when my Hermit teacher first introduced me to all of this, I thought it was all rather ridiculous and it took me quite some time before I came around to the idea of all of this, let alone start applying it to myself. If I was living in some religious bias bubble of comfort, I would have waved these teachings off, as many do. But I was in the Dark Night of the Soul and this was my only way out of that, so in a sense, there was no choice.

When I came across the question: 'Is the thought of something, the same as the actual something? Is the thought of a rock, the same as an actual rock? Etc.' It was really a subtle yet deep and profound Eureka moment! It was something really simple, but I never really ever questioned it in the beginning, and when I did question and examine this premise, the next logical question was: 'Am I who I think I am?' This is what the teachings are all about and boil down to and a number of levels.

I also receive quite a few e-mails from people who are just starting out in their 'belief system' and everything that comes with that. Surely there is a place and time for everyone to go through those steps, but what is being taught & presented here, is for those in the last stages towards Union. People who are just starting out with 'Religion' that read these exchanges, have e-mailed me and told me none of it makes any sense, so there's sort of a built in filter if that makes sense. People's own ability to understand, filters them from higher understanding, until they are ready one day.

I've come across way too many personality types, or rather anti-personalities to this methodology. They're just too many to list. But to give you some examples there's all the folks with Attention Deficit Disorder, which our modern day society seems to create a lot of. These people can't stay focused on single book page, let alone a YouTube video. So meditation is out of the question. You also have the typical 'seeking addict', which is a person who is addicted to seeking and reading about more and more information and content. For such a person, it's not about applying any of what is taught here, but only to gather mentally the philosophy of what is being said, and to set it aside in the mental collection of all the other philosophies that are out there to be sought.

All that being said, there are plenty of people who won't get this and some who originally didn't, until a later time when they returned to e-mail or see me and stated that something shifted for them to be able to understand what is being said here.

Question: I had a momentary glimpse of Union. How do I go back there and what do I do to make it return?

Answer: The 'Union Glimpse' occurs spontaneously and on its own as a fruition of all of this investigation into, and letting go all identities.

Trying to "get back there" and "doing" anything to get it back is recreating another identity that get's in the way of Union. The glimpse, came, the glimpse left, and all that's left now is a continuation of non-identifying, loose surrender, letting go, not grasping or clinging to any identities and allowing this whole No Self Atmosphere to deepen so that it takes on a life of its own, and allows Union to eventually re-manifest again.

Question: Everything feels neutral or sort of dead from practicing the No Self Atmosphere. Is this normal?

Answer: Yes, very normal. True reality itself has an aspect of neutrality to it, in that it is a pure potential from which anything can manifest, be it good or bad. God is pure potentiality, amongst an infinite number of other aspects, and this pure potentiality has an aspect of neutrality to it, which many people label as a deadness.

That neutrality is the perfect platform from which to disidentify all the aspects that the ego believes to be a 'you'. If you are no longer identifying with anything from a place, or identifier of 'unidentifier,' then that identifier is still an identity. But if doing so from neutrality, that has a better chance of not having any identities there from which to no longer identify with.

Later as life comes to pass, that neutrality can be used to pass through what others see as the difficulties in life. For example if a loved one passes, or some harsh words are said about the apparent you, or a job is lost, then the neutrality is there for the sake of allowing an unbiased look at the situation, instead of an identified one with bias, and clinging, and freaking out. Not that any of those are wrong per se, as its perfectly normal to grieve for a loved one, be sad about job loss, and so forth. However, knowing that the loved one isn't that meat suit that just passed, and that you also aren't this current meat suit, allows the neutrality and a knowing, that there will be a reunification with that later apparent individual in another form, and that's just one of many ways of looking at reality.

The deadness can also be balanced with a subtle love, joy, and/or happiness as an aspect of the No Self Atmosphere. Anything that takes away from either or all of those aspects, shows you that you are being identified with something that is getting in the way of the No Self Atmosphere, and can then be disidentified from, so there is a return to those aspects that are part of No Self. This can all be cultivated in one of two ways; The No Self Atmosphere, or the No Self Atmosphere of all pervading Love.

Question: I feel like there is so much crap there to spring clean within me and I don't know if I'll ever get to the bottom of the crap pile to uncover what's behind it all. How do I go about dealing with all of this?

Answer: Don't identify with any of it, and don't identify with an 'I' that owns any of it or has to do anything about it. If the 'I' is seen as simply an imagined belief, a shadow, a daydream, an illusion, and you spend more and more time choosing to no longer believe in it, then it will fall away along with all the crap. Even after that, 'crap' may still seem to appear, but none of it is yours, none of it is real, all of it can be instantaneously surrendered and let go of that moment it appears. So have a laugh and take a sigh of relief, because we are not going down the road of claiming anything or ownership of anything. It's quite the opposite; giving it all away and no longer owning anything so that the inherent freedom that is already there can shine brilliantly of its own accord in everyday life.

Question: I'm currently at a point of dealing with the fear of how life will be if there really is no me. I've read how the others in the exchanges dealt with it, but for some reason can't seem to make it apply to myself. How do I go about this?

Answer: Dealing with this existential fear is a really good place to be, because it is one of the last and greatest tricks the ego uses to perpetuate it's unreal and false self. To be quite blunt, it just has to be gone through and faced no matter how long it takes and no matter how unpleasant it can be.

For some people, they simply say, "What have I got to lose, it can't be as bad as Egoic life," and the rest is history. These people have a point. That fear is the border between living a selfless life of Union, and living the old Egoic status quo. So if you don't face it and go through it, then you are right back in the Egoic illusion life.

Different people deal with it differently, but my biggest recommendation is to befriend it, spend time with it, examine it, and get to know it. Then by doing so, there is a comfort that comes with knowing that this fear isn't real, is illogical, is an illusion, is an emotion playing itself out as a daydream, and that the 'you' which also isn't real, is identifying with this unreal fear. The more all of that which I just wrote is seen and gotten used to, the quicker and easier it will be.

Question: I think I may have had an experience of the ego-ungluing that you speak of. It's like the place and position of all the thoughts that identify as me, shifted to another further location than where it used to be, and I was separate from it. Is this the ungluing you speak of?

Answer: Yes, the ego ungluing which happens after X amount of time of no longer identifying with it, manifests in a myriad of ways with a myriad of phenomena from both my own experience and the dozens of correspondences that I have had with people who have successfully undone themselves through this methodology.

It sounds like it's a first ungluing experience, and this is usually followed up by a return to continuing to identify with the ego, for most people. Quite a few folks have to go through several of these ungluing experiences before it becomes permanent and Union manifests.

Also, as I'm sure you've noticed, during that ungluing experience, that same ego is also commenting on its own ungluing, trying to trick 'you' by making 'you' identify with what's happening, as something that's happening to this apparent 'you.' That's some very sneaky and crafty trickery performed by the ego and it has to be known that this is one of its continued illusions.

So for the ungluing to be permanent, it has to be established as the experiential norm for quite some time, along with the disidentification and letting go of any of the additional Egoic commentary that plays out with the ungluing process.

Question: I was just wondering if this is something I can come back to at a later time? I'm currently a Mother of three kids and run a daycare business with my husband that requires me to wear all these different hats all day long. I feel like giving up all these identities will prevent me from being on my A-game for all that needs be done. Is that okay?

Answer: Sure it's okay, and of the hundreds of emails I've received and people I've worked with, quite a few admit that they're not ready to go through this just yet, and that's fine.

Just remember that you already undo and let go of all identities every night during the process of falling asleep, except that it's done so unconsciously. Adding conscious awareness to the process doesn't take that much in the beginning stages of this whole process.

Also remember that being in Union, makes it so much easier to go through a hectic lifestyle because it's like being on autopilot. You're still doing and staying on top of all the things that need to be done and taken care of, but it's all seen and experienced as one massive and united flow with no 'you' in the way of it.

Also, ask yourself where your original question is coming from and whether or not it's from fear of the unknown, from fear of Union, from Ego itself. Remember, the ego is a crafty excuse maker, and I've worked with people who had some of the craziest schedules you can imagine who have successfully figured out how to work this process into their busy lives in a way where Union has manifested.

Question: I understand all of this intellectually, but how can I make this an experience?

Answer: See that 'experience' is already happening, and is the first primary function of apparent 'reality.' So first there was the 'experience' of reading this book and/or watching/listening to the videos. That resulted in the 'experience' of 'understanding this intellectually.' That, in turn, has produced this desire to make what is being understood intellectually, an actual experience. 'Experience' itself is already happening, so now you have to examine to see and ask 'what does it consist of?' Upon examination you'll find feelings, thoughts, a body, senses, and so forth. So now, all that has to be done, is a systematic seeing/perception/awareness, that whatever makes up 'experiencing' is happening on its own, without a 'you' doing it. That goes for every single aspect of experience that you find; all senses, all thoughts, emotions, movements, actions, perception, awareness, etc.

So there already is 'an experience' happening. Get in touch with experience and start deconstructing it so it's all going on, by itself, no 'you' anywhere to be found. The exchanges read and re-read will produce the insights needed to keep this going forward, and the meditations of the No Self Atmosphere and A.M./P.M mediations will do the rest.

Question: I started doing the meditations and applying the exchanges to my own experience, but I lost the steam because of work and family and life stuff in general. I feel like I know what this is all about, but there's just no time to do it. How can I get back into it?

Answer: The time simply has to be found for this, and as seen in Adam's exchange, every single event of the day, to varying degrees, can incorporate this work no matter how busy you are. There are times of the day that are prone for more depth for this, commute/travel, lunch breaks, first 20 minutes of the day and last 20 minutes of the night, and so forth. Really the onus is on you to find the time to do so. I ask of everyone who undertakes this methodology to really minimize all aspects of their life. For example less social media/internet/television, less going out, less socializing, and sacrificing the time that would otherwise be spent in useless endeavors, for the sake of something grand, something that's more important, and that's Union with God.

You have to be 100% honest and genuine with yourself about going through this, or else the ego will find all the clever and unseen justifications in the world to minimize anything that has to do with this, and maximize everything that has to do with itself.

I will leave you with an interesting observation that you can use to honestly ask yourself where you stand with all of this. I have a handful of people e-mail or call me everyday who come across this work and are interested in Union, and they always fall into one of three categories. The first one of which I call the window shoppers. These are people who get interested in all of this for a bit, a few days or weeks, but then disappear, never to be seen or heard from again. The second group, I call the procrastinators, most of who dive into all these teachings on an intellectual understanding level, might do some meditations here and there, but return to the life distractions and Egoic identities. Some return eventually and follow through to Union, but they are very few and far between. The last group, are those who take this and run with it until Union manifests, and they are the 1%'ers. These are people who make this a living and breathing part of their daily lives, so much so, that it's just a matter of time before Union dawns. For these folks, there is no other choice but to go through with it no matter the sacrifices.

So ask yourself, honestly, which category are you, and if it's worth continuing down the status quo of your current mode of life for whatever gains are there, for whatever reasons it is that this whole Union business has been set on the side? Is it worth Union with God?

When Christ said to "be in the world, but not of it," he spoke volumes of the nature of this existence, this realm, all in those few words. Our western society is constructed in a way specifically so that you don't have the time to think critically and deconstruct the ego, so that the majority of waking hours are spent externally doing, getting, chasing, making, working, saving, seeking, etc. But this work consists of undoing, non-being, allowing, surrendering, and so forth, and that creates quite the schism to find one's way through.

So it's really up to you to take responsibility for all of this and find the time for it wherever it may be, or consider a self retreat, a camping trip in solitude, or doing a retreat with me.

For me, it was really enough just to understand the unreality of the ego and to spend those last 15-30 minutes while laying in bed at night and waiting for sleep to takeover, to really dive in deep into all of this and examine those last vestiges of the ego that play out at the end of the day. Genuinely seeing how all those stories are playing out and how they don't have to be believed any more. The longer and deeper the 'unbelief' of the ego went, the quicker it became unglued and it's illusion based unreality fell away.

Question: Can you give me a simplified breakdown of where Union happens to someone who hasn't yet become a Christian, but is considering becoming one? I've watched your Stages of Spiritual experiences video (not sure if that's the exact title of it) and I'm wondering if you can expand on this.

Answer: That's a pretty big question and is a philosophical can of worms which has volumes of books written on it in terms of the Union experience and theology written about it. I know people who have lived Union experiences in their childhood prior to being told about any religions. And others who have had spontaneous glimpses of Union while raking leaves, making love to their significant other, or riding a bike in the park while they were agnostics or atheists, though soon after those experiences, they've told me their old positions and beliefs began to fade in terms of Atheism/Agnosticism.

So the Union experience is or can be, arguably, different from what entails all the mystical experience within the path of following the teachings of Christ. However, the Union experience via the Theosis/Deification process, is an integral part of the Eastern and Orthodox Christianities and of Jesus himself.

In terms of the stages for a Christian, paraphrased would be as follows.

A person gets interested in Christianity (regardless of denomination), gets involved in some sort of community, Bible study, services, listening to sermons and so forth.

This starts the practices of prayer, repentance, love, change, growth spiritually in terms of faith, trust, love, and practice daily the activation of these various, as of before unused, faculties.

This creates a connection to Christ that eventually becomes palpable and there can begin to be felt a reciprocation of love, peace, change and other attributes over time and growth.

This relationship to the beings of Christ & God, which initially seems far and distant, are constantly cultivated and grown to a point of full saturation of your own being, so that the distance and farness don't seem to be there anymore.

Eventually, you undergo a baptism, or re-baptism if you had one as a newborn, and this water ritual gives the signal for the Holy Spirit to come and eventually indwell you, killing off the ego and replacing it with higher spiritual faculties such as bliss, transcendence, empathy, love for all beings, non-judgment, openness, peace, ease of transcending the animalistic tendencies of the body, and many other 'gifts of the Spirit.'

This period of being indwelled by the Spirit, or as some call it, 'slain by the Spirit' (as in the slaying of the ego) can last anywhere from an hour all the way and up to many years, but eventually for people on the road to Union there comes a period called the Dark Night of the Soul.

Not everyone has to go through it, but it manifests for the sake of Spring cleaning the rest of what's left of this belief that there is a 'you' separate from God. The Dark Night is also the birth of a deep access to your own Being, a Beingness so richly dynamic and it goes very deeply within, where it eventually merges with God's being in Union. 'Beingness' is prior to all thoughts, emotions, consciousness, and so forth, it is like the ground if which all things happen on.

So after traversing the Dark Night, the next stop is Union with God, and even after that happens, there is literally no end to the ways in which Union evolves.

As to the term 'Christian,' it's just a label, a word that was given by non-Christians to those who were following the Way to Union which Jesus taught. They were originally called, 'followers of the Way,' and what happens if you follow a certain way to somewhere, is that you eventually reach the destination and experience it for yourself, even if that experience is that there is no self in the infinite Omnipresent totality of it all.

Question: I have an easy time with this whole Union business during the quiet and still times of my day when I'm applying these teachings. But soon as I get into activities such as talking, jogging, movement, and general social situations is when I get caught back up into the story of this 'me.' Is there anything I can do to get a better grip on this lack of integration into movement?

Answer: You have to bring everything you have learned from these teachings into movement, consciously, aware, and actively so that a new habit is created that allows all the old habitual identifications to fall away. So for example, when jogging, the jog is happening on its own. All the senses are united and are happening on their own. The mind will create the stream of illusions and kidnap attention, so a continuous return to no longer believing that stream of thoughts. Making it a habit to see if you can go the whole jog with the unbelief of the thought streams and identities in place, along with the seeing and feeling that the whole jog is happening on its own. Also start incorporating this into all other actions as well, such as showering, laundry, cooking, eating, and so forth.

Talking with others is a tough one, because the habitual illusion and subtle daydream of 'me and others' comes into play and it's certainly one of the more challenging deconstructions to go through, however it is also doable. The key is to stay aware and conscious of the engagement in communications. Notice how the body tenses up when talking and how there is a loss of awareness out into the external reality of the engagement.

So you want to reverse this process by making sure there is no tightness anywhere physically going on, a sort of looseness is there for the whole body. Along with this there should be an openness to seeing the whole interaction as one massive living thing with no separation or division. Instead of harboring the idea that 'I'm talking to this person about whatever topics,' it should be more of a taking in the whole omnipresence of the whole event. There are all these senses going on in the room, the colors, breathing, feeling, listening, talking, perhaps there or more people coming and going, the temperature, and so forth. Reality is rich and dynamic and it's One united massive living Beingness, so just by keeping that in mind and allowing yourself to be in a loose and surrendered state of being, it can and eventually will be enough for Union to manifest in these sorts of active situations.

The biggest thing to take away from all this is that you have within you X amount of years of habitual illusion programming, so to see through it all as illusion, for many people doesn't happen overnight. Though it does for some, and even those who see it instantly, they too revert back to the old tendencies. So there will be a spring cleaning of illusion based views that goes on for however long a person needs, to be permanently living in a place of Union which itself has no views, is dynamic, transcendent, beyond any positions and limits.

Question: I'm getting to a place where I'm starting to deconstruct all dualities and opposites and I guess I'm seeing through them, or rather past them in some strange and transcendent way. Can you speak more on that? I've already had some deep and lengthy glimpses of the Union experience, but this seems to be something deeper if that makes sense. Am I on the right track?

Answer: Yes of course that's all part of it and I will speak more on this and provide a list in a second book of more in depth exchanges. It's merely the logical next step in this process to undo and unravel the dualities that the ego believes in and you are on the right track.

We see the inside of our home as 'inside,' and the birds nested on the branch as 'outside.' But for the birds, they are 'inside' and we are 'outside.' Or we see the sky as 'up' and the ground as 'down,' however neither the ground nor the sky have these ideas of up or down, nor do the birds that simply fly with the flow of the wind the blows beneath them, try and ask a bird what 'wind' is and see what kind of answer you get.

So we can look at, say for example 'inside vs. outside,' as a duality and argue it philosophically that is true, isn't true, is both true and not true, or none of the above. But we are not here to argue and debate, but rather to undo and deconstruct so that Union in all its fullness can manifest and show experientially that everything is United and One.

There is a massive list of the dualities to deconstruct, but this can turn into another identity of 'I have to get this list and I have to deconstruct it.' We are not going that route, but instead can use daily experiences in life's setting to watch and see the illusions that arise so they can be no longer believed and seen through on the spot, as they occur. However, going the other route and looking at such a list can also be helpful. I actually do this at some retreats, covering some simple differences, or dualities, and asking the retreatants if inside vs. outside really exists if it's not thought about. If you look in a room with an opened window, that whole process of seeing is primarily naked, and then just milliseconds after the initial sense of seeing is occurring, the mind comes in with all these labels and thoughts such as, "Hmmm, I wonder who left the window to the outside open." So we're catching this inner commentator and resting in the nakedness of existence just prior to any comments being made. You're on the right track!

Question: Can you go more in depth on what it means to understand this teaching in terms of intuition, feelings, and some of the other descriptions you went into? I get everything I've read so far and I'm applying it, but I guess I'm having trouble with making the teachings go deeper to this intuitive and felt level.

Answer: Quite a few people aren't connected deeply to their intuition, however almost everyone I've ever spoken with about this topic has had experiences in the past where they've intuited something and it ended up being right. Whether it was premonitions about a person being good or bad, or deciding for or against some life choice that ends up being the correct choice to have made in retrospect, pretty much everyone has the built in ability.

To apply these teachings intuitively, means to simply feel them from that deeper level. For example, you can have an intellectual understanding that all the senses are all happening at the same time and it makes sense logically. However before you even check and see for yourself if this is true, you already have this feeling that this is more than likely true. Or in another example, it makes sense intellectually that the thought of a rock is not an actual rock, and from there on out, you have this intuitive sense to investigate whether this is so further, you have to spend some time contemplating the two. You can actually go and find a rock, hold it in your hand, and feel the rock, and see the thought of that rock in your mind, examining and feeling the difference between the two from a deeper felt & contemplative level.

The act of contemplating things deeper is intuitive intelligence and what I'm asking you to do is to get on a bike and ride it so you know how to balance it, steer, pedal in such a way so that you eventually let go of the handle bars and drift into Union. If the intuitive knowledge of the experience isn't there, then all you have is the intellectual understanding of what it must be like to ride a bike.

Question: I've been having some strange experiences since I started practicing the YouTube meditations and following the exchanges. I wouldn't exactly call them Union experiences because there is still a 'me' in them, but for certain stretches of time everything becomes hyperrealism. I don't really know any other way to put it, but I haven't seen this mentioned in any of the other exchanges. Is this normal?

Answer: Yes it's quite normal actually. People call these shifts and experiences by differing terms and 'hyperrealism' certainly fits into it. There are a myriad of phenomena that will occur as one get's used to living a selfless life. Don't hold on to any of it, identify with any of it, or identify with a 'me' who is trying to get back to the 'hyperrealism.' Just continuing to no longer believe the ego is real and a further deconstruction and surrender into the No Self Atmosphere will suffice.

Question: I recently got into a debate with a friend that turned into a heated argument based on your teachings. It's so plain to see how true all of this is, but he just doesn't get it and is basically sleepwalking through life with an Egoic lifestyle. Does this have to be such a lonely path or can I share this with others who will get it?

Answer: There's a lot of labeling going on in your statement in terms of duality and division. Ultimately there is no such thing as sleepwalking, ego, and so on in the Oneness of God's Union. It may feel like a lonely path, but there is no such thing as 'alone,' which is just another mental daydream construct. Life is all around that apparent 'you' and there is never a time or place where you are alone and away from life itself.

The tendency to shout these teachings out from the rooftops is also another identity and self imposed Egoic construct. Allow Union to manifest directly and permanently and then people around you will know that something has changed and might be more receptive. However, coming out as some sort of ego destroyer will simply be threatening to people's ego's and they can or will respond malevolently, knowing themselves intuitively, though mostly entirely unconscious of the fact, that these teachings do culminate in ego death.

Also, there's no need to debate or argue. The play of a person believing they are the ego and body and them not having the ability to understand or comprehend this, is just an appearance, a single appearance of the Oneness of God. If you take that one appearance to be the totality then you're missing the wholeness of what's really going on. What I've done in the past is drop subtle hints, sort of plant seeds to family, friends, and loved ones. Whenever they're ready to talk, then I'd be there for them to take things further.

Question: As far as the minimalism you ask people to undertake who are starting with these teachings, are books okay? Because I usually jump between several books during the week depending on what mood I'm in and never really stick to one to the end.

Question: No other books or reading materials, limited television, internet, seeking, occupying yourself with distractions. You have to put yourself fully and completely into this with one pointed concentration as much as possible. It's like digging one deep well to get to the water, instead of digging a bunch of shallow wells and never reaching the water. All these books you jump between are the shallow wells.

The majority of people that contact me and read the exchanges are window shoppers, they're merely passing through to check out what's here, and off they go in their retained egotism.

If you want this to work, it's more like entering the shop and boarding yourself in completely with the notion that the 'you' that you take yourself to be, will die here in this shop and all the focus will be on this death. The window shoppers continue to come and go, but you're staying until it's done and over with.

Question: I'm very active in my life and am a leader in my community and Church, which means I help a lot of people and always busy doing something. Since I've started reading the exchanges, I've realized I'm really imbalanced in terms of meditation because of my busy lifestyle. How do I overcome this resistance to simply being with these meditations when I'm constantly doing something?

Answer: Yes, there is clearly an imbalance between being and doing. Basically, jump right into the No Self Atmosphere mediation and get used to it. There will be a ton of resistance and excuses that the ego creates to not go through with this. So these all have to be seen for what they are, unreal illusions and blockages to Union, and then they have to be overcome by allowing yourself to continue to sit through all of it. There should be a falling in love with this whole process, a sweetness, a looking forward to undoing all of the programs and habits and a curiosity to see what happens when Union manifests. Sure, eventually even everything I just said is surrendered and let go of, however it's enough to go on in the beginning.

It's like learning to ride a bike or going to the gym for the first time. Seems daunting at first, but the more you workout, the more you feel and see the difference.

Question: I work as a computer programmer and coder. Could this process be described as a sort of mental reprogramming?

Answer: Yes this exactly what is going on here. We are programmed from birth in terms of made up language and concepts which cause us to eventually live in a mental prison made up of biases and extremely limited views. If you use the internet to research the term 'list of cognitive biases,' you'll come across a list of over 100+ biases that exist in people which skews the view of reality and blocks access to Union, and that's just covering cognitive biases. With new scientific findings coming to the surface daily, we have groups of other biases that are still as of yet unknown as far as how they function in us. Epigenetics, for example, is a branch of science that studies genetics that are inherited from both parents and how that affects the individual person. There are a ton of studies coming out in animal models that learned behavior, fear, and other phenomena can be passed down to the next generation. How that translates to humans is still being studied and debated, however we have to then keep into account the number of epigenetic biases that are passed down into us.

We also have a number of relativities in terms of having more or less intelligence, situational awareness, intuition, emotional intelligence, and so forth. Each of the aforementioned factors can cause a number of biases based on having less or more of each compared to others.

So we are, in effect, deprogramming all of these factors by no longer identifying with any of them and reaching a pre programmed stated of being. It is this pre programmed state which gives us access to the source of life, of existence, of consciousness, of Union itself.

Question: Reading these exchanges as a Roman Catholic is quite an eye opener. I've come to realize that I used my religion to create another identity. It's also made me quite bitter and judgmental towards anything that isn't part of my belief system and I've probably gotten a bigger ego because of it. How do I reconcile having my Religion while letting go of my identity that's based on it?

Answer: This is exactly what systematic religion does to people, is it creates another identity, or what I call the Christian Ego, or rather to word it more universally, it would be a religious ego.

If you read your Bible, Jesus wasn't forming churches or starting any religions. In fact, he was debating and arguing with the leaders of Jewish religions and breaking many of their long held rules and beliefs. Amongst many other things, he was a vagabond teacher of Mystical Union with God, and we have no record of him asking his followers to start Churches and denominations.

We also have records of Catholic hermits, mystics, and monks who have experienced Union with God and have spoken about it extensively, which shows that this heart and core of experiential Union exists within Catholicism.

Once I entered into Christianity, I noticed myself also taking on the views of those around me and I eventually became much more judgmental and biased against anything that wasn't like what I believed or how I viewed things. Considering Jesus teaches ego death, instead of my ego dying, I had instead traded my old worldly ego, for a Christian Ego which justified worldly activities under the guise that I'll be alright and be forgiven as long as I repent.

Eventually receiving the indwelling of the Holy Spirit, the whole construct of my ego was shattered into a million pieces as if slain and no longer existing. I was from then on, completely like a newborn child with no filters, no judgments, no views except pure and utter Love and Bliss.

It was this experience and help from a number of Monks, Mystics, and a non-denominational Hermit which helped me to realize that Union comes about by no longer identifying with any identity. By seeing that these identities are imagined, are not real, are illusions, and letting them go, allows for an opening into the purest form of surrender which leads to Union, and having worked with quite a number of people in this respect, the Union experience is repeatable.

Of the many Catholics I've worked with, they still continue to go to their services and take their sacraments; however it's all done from a place of non-identification, non-doing, allowing, flow, love, and simplicity from the elements that manifest in the Atmosphere of No Self Meditations. This deepens the experience of the ultimate meaning of Church services and the sacraments especially experiencing them from the omnipresence of Union.

Question: I'm an agnostic and one of my Christian friends sent me a pdf of your book which I've been deeply digging into and so far it's simply amazing. A lot of what I'm reading just seems like common sense, and not necessarily religious or Christian based. I don't necessarily have to be a Christian to get any of this right? I have a lot of resistance towards religions and disagree with a large portion of the Old Testament, but what I'm reading so far has been great!

Answer: No, you don't have to be a 'Christian' to get any of this. I know an individual who was in Union for their entire childhood. And another person, a self professed agnostic, who glimpsed the Union experience while riding their bike in the park one day. The people I work with locally and at retreats come from diverse backgrounds and some aren't Christians.

However, both of these aforementioned people eventually came to see the truth of Jesus' teachings as pointers towards the Union experience as the underlying reality of all things and have since established a connection to these teachings.

You can be a Christian and go through a vast array of mystical changes, gained spiritual faculties, and other interesting phenomena, and yet not be in Union with God. You can also be in the Union experience, and have yet to have gained the mystical changes, spiritual faculties, and graces that come from connecting to the teachings of Christ. You can also have both of these, or also lack both of these situations. There also as many differing and relative scenarios of what I stated above, as there are people, however the important thing is to keep going into the directions you're headed in. Reading Blueprints to Union is already enough to make you start questioning everything.

Those resistances to anything religious you speak of make complete sense because I was once an Atheist and also held these same views amongst many others. However the Union experience changes everything. You no longer see things from limits, logic, and reason, but instead tap into the ability to see in a transcendent and unlimited manner.

Also, we aren't born with any beliefs, and as we grow up, we start to take more and more of them on. This whole process is to go beyond any beliefs and to experience Union directly. That Union experience transcends beliefs because it exists prior to any beliefs. Beliefs can come and go, but they come and go within Union, which doesn't go away as the ultimate and supreme reality in which all things happen.

Question: This is such a revolutionary book to me, I feel like I'm freed from the prison that my Church put me in and I'm starting to have some serious experiences with this. How do I tell others at the Church considering this basically destroys their 'Churchy' egos? I feel like a spy when I'm there now, like I figured out the ultimate key to Union, but I can't share it with anyone there because they're so limited by their own denomination.

Answer: Don't worry about others for now. Just continue in the unraveling and ego ungluing to the point of Union manifesting and being integrated. This is very common to many people I've worked with. They keep their Mystical path secret from the rest of the Church members, and for the most part everyone, and this is how it's supposed to be as it's even stated in Christian scripture:

Matthew 6:6 "But when you pray, go into your room, close the door and pray to your Father, who is unseen. Then your Father, who sees what is done in secret, will reward you."

So you are technically cultivating the Egoic unraveling and undoing in secret. It's a purification of the heart, so that Union can manifest and it's all done secretly. Furthermore we have this verse:

Matthew 5:8 "Blessed are the pure of heart, for they shall see God."

The heart is impure due to the ego and all of its constructs; the belief in the I-Thought(I, me, mine), the belief in dualities(me vs. others, up vs. down, here vs. there, me here vs. God there), the belief in divisions and separations, the belief that the body is you, and so forth. When all of this is seen through as unreal, as daydream based superimpositions, and when it is all systematically surrendered and given up, then we are secretly entering into the purity of the heart where God can be seen.

It will be up to your intuition on who to share this with and how to do it. If anything, give them a copy of the book and see what they say. You can just leave it open ended by saying something to the extent of, "Hey friend, I recently read this book and still don't know what to think of it. Maybe you can share some feedback with me." This will usually give you a good indication of where the person is. If they throw it back in your face and tell you that it's all the work of the devil, then most likely you have a fundamentalist on your hands with hardened heart based on the Fundamentalist ego construct.

Sometimes, people come across these teachings during a time when they are still in a place of limited intelligence and fairly early in their spiritual walk, and in many cases they'll return later to reexamine this material when there is a maturity of intuition and intelligence.

You have to understand, there is a self filtering mechanism at play here. The person's own ego will filter whether or not there is an openness and availability to allow the ego to die and enter into Union. So no matter how this is presented and to whom, the intelligence of Union itself will decide whose spiritual eyes can be opened and when in terms of entering into Union.

Question: So I've already started the meditations and deconstructions and was wondering if there is any kind of map or signposts to look for along the way to Union. Am I looking for anything specific as I go through this process?

Answer: I have considered providing some general signposts along the way to Union, however after working with people for the last 5 years with this specific methodology, there is simply too much ambiguity amongst different people and the different sorts of phenomena and experiences that arise from this method. At the same time, there are Universalities as well and I will try to post some examples and also give a bottom line.

An ambiguity would be in the ungluing of the ego experience. When there is a developed continuous seeing and being aware of the ego, the trains of thoughts, the 'I, me, mine' constructs and everything that they wrap themselves up in, eventually you bring a subset of tools to deconstruct, no longer believe in, and no longer identify with all that I just mentioned. This will bring about the ungluing of the ego experience which happens prior to Union.

This ungluing is different for different people. For some, nothing really changes and everything remains the same except for noticing that there no longer is any identification going on with any of the egotism. Some people have dramatic experiences where the ego is seen and experienced in way as if it has been removed and taken off like a mask floating in mid air, while being able to clearly witness it from a distance. Some people end up seeing the ego from the very first moment that it arises in the morning and they comment that it's like a swarm of flies, each fly being a certain Egoic construct. For some, the place where the ego seems to take place shifts to the side of the head, or to different places within the head or body area. Sometimes people will be called by their names and have to remind themselves that the name refers to this body that other people take to be you, so there can be a delay to responding to words, labels, names as everything is surrendered and reprogrammed.

In terms of the Union experience, it has universal traits such as the dissolution of any boundaries, divisions, separations. You no longer feel yourself to be limited to the body or to the mind, and experience a unity with everything around you. That unity is boundless, omnipresent, living, conscious, and many other factors that everyone is agreeing on. However, many of the subset sub experiences that come with Union can also differ. For some Union coexists with and is made of Love, or light, or both and for others it's more a spaciousness that lacks Love and the Love comes much later since Union also evolves and grows and changes over time.

Regardless, the signposts are various and the goal is Union, however the bottom line is not to cling to any goals or to look for any signposts because by doing so, you are recreating and re-identifying with a subtle Egoic I-construct. These signposts, changes, ego ungluing, and eventual Union, all come about of their own accord in time just simply by undergoing and applying to yourself all of these teachings.

Question: I just watched your video on the mechanics of the ego and you mentioned something about our consciousness being imprisoned by the ego. Is this what we're doing here is basically freeing our consciousness from this self imposed prison?

Answer: As a short answer, yes this is so. In Union, your consciousness unifies with God's consciousness and results in the Union experience. What's preventing that from happening is the habitual attachment to thoughts and beliefs in terms of identities, divisions, separations, limits, and so on.

A really big secret to all of this, a sort of shortcut, is to realize that there is no one who is imprisoned. Sure there may be all these thoughts, illusions, daydreams, and identifications that are habitually being identified with, however just contemplating that everything is happening on its own and there is no 'you' to whom its happening to, can be enough for Union to manifest. It's almost like a Bowl believing that it's a goldfish within a bowl, but the bowl is empty and there is no goldfish. The bowl and goldfish were merely being believed in to be true, but beliefs are insubstantial illusion daydreams.

The prison falls away and dissolves when it's no longer believed in. However getting to this point takes a number of steps. If I asked you to sit down for 10 minutes and write down all the streams of thought that occur one after another, and give me this list, it would be an initial step in becoming aware of the habitual tendencies of the ego constructs. Then we can discuss them and break them all down. So the first step is becoming consciously aware throughout the day of the prison bars, which are the streams of thought and all the views, opinions, judgments which we are filtering reality through.

Once you become aware of them, you can realize they are just daydreams that you are choosing to believe in, but can now choose to no longer believe in. Furthermore then, you can choose to longer believe that there is a 'you.' This is how it starts and eventually deepens so that the prison becomes unglued. The biggest belief that we are undoing is the belief that there is a separate you. Once that belief in a separate you is no longer believed in, the corresponding surrender and letting go existentially will open the doors to the Union experience.

Question: I'm not sure if it was in the exchanges or one of your videos, but you mentioned getting your attention to rest in itself. Is this where we are surrendering from and can you tell me exactly how one surrenders?

Answer: Yes, we want attention to rest in itself, because attention is usually leaking outwardly and being imprisoned and filtered by egotism. So that habitual process of always sending attention outward, needs to be reversed so that it can return into itself and rest there, completely detached from any ego identities, beliefs, imagination, and any day dreams or thought streams.

Surrender is something that happens every night when the body is falling asleep, except that it happens unconsciously. Just by entering into sleep consciously and aware, we can start to study and examine what happens. The body relaxes, all physical tension is being loosened and surrendered, we are letting go of all the worries and thoughts of the day and of what tomorrow brings, and resting into this slow surrender into sleep.

So falling asleep is your direct experiential teacher which is giving you a lesson in surrender every single night. Once you stay aware and conscious of that process over a few days or a week, then you can apply that same surrender in the No Self Atmosphere mediation, except that in that meditation, we are first detaching and disidentifying from thoughts, senses, and the body in order for attention to rest in itself and be able to be surrendered downward. Also, surrender has to be done consciously, without falling asleep.

After a while and some practice, you can get used to attention itself and how it has the ability to be attentive to any one object, location, direction and so forth, and then how to let go of all of those externalities and to simply reverse attention so it's attentive to itself. In other words, putting attention on attention itself and allowing it to rest in that way, entirely detached from anything else.

Question: I guess I can say I'm in some weird place with all of this. Like I read all the exchanges and I completely get what this is all about, but since I get it and I figured it out intellectually, I have no other interest in pursuing this any further. I almost feel like I'm tricking myself through some sort of Egoic self justification and excuses. What do I do?

Answer: Well, you've figured out exactly what's going on and stated it plainly. It clearly is an Egoic trick to figure something out and construct a sort of intellectual contentment and satiation. It's an Egoic constructed that basically says, "I got this all figured out and understood and now I'm off to other things." This usually results in moving on to other books, other areas of interests, other teachings, and yet completely disregarding the practical and experiential part of this teaching that leads to its fruition in Union.

This is simply an Egoic resistance, and you have to face it and sit with it. If it can be overcome, then the next step is to start applying the teachings by going into the Atmosphere of No Self Mediation, and the A.M./P.M. meditations. This has to be repeated daily and a continued deconstruction of the ego throughout the day so it builds up steam and starts to produce fruit.

Some people who have come to some of the retreats have told me that they forced themselves to the retreats because there were too many resistances of various sorts that stood in the way of going through with this. The majority of people who contact me about all of this, whom I call window shoppers, people who check out the videos and the exchanges, and then go about their old ways, basically don't stick around because of the resistances and trickery that the ego creates. So to a certain degree, it's up to you to get this going so that you reach a point where it's clearly seen that there is no more you and Union manifests.

Question: You said that you went through ego death from the indwelling of the Holy Spirit. If that's the case, then shouldn't we seek ego death that way instead of the way you're teaching here?

Answer: Before I went through ego death via the Holy Spirit through the Christian teachings, I ended up harboring a number of Christian, religious, and denominational based ego constructs that did not necessarily help in ego death. Some of the Egoic constructs were very vapid and decisive based, especially when I started studying and debating all the different denominations and having debates about them with my Bible study teacher and those around me.

To a certain degree, I was able to let go of many of those ego identities and simply Love whatever I thought God was, Christ, and the Holy Spirit and with a rebaptism, it was enough to trigger the indwelling of the Holy Spirit leading to ego death, or from what I would call from here on out as ego death by grace.

These teachings, on the other hand, is an entrance to ego death via wisdom and knowledge, which eventually trigger grace as well. The grace opens access to the Union experience, however you are getting to the point by cultivating that wisdom and knowledge that the 'you' who you believe yourself to be, is merely an illusion based phantom, like a belief in Santa Claus.

If you're better suited towards one way versus the other, then by all means go that route. However if you combine the two methodologies, they compound each other and strengthen and quicken the whole ego Death process.

So it can happen through Holy Spirit indwelling , or through wisdom/knowledge, or through both combined. However I will note that even after my ego death experience via the Holy Spirit indwelling, I did still recreate and cling to many of the old Egoic and worldly constructs, and by all means I needed to have access to these teachings from my Hermit teacher in order for Union to come about. So for me it was a combination of the two, however for many people that I work with, Union comes about primarily through the wisdom/knowledge self application of these teachings.

Question: I feel like I have to go to a retreat or somewhere else in order to start this process, which I know is silly if I think about it. It's quite an absurd idea and I'm guessing you will say let go of this, am I right?

Answer: A retreat atmosphere is certainly beneficial to deepen the whole process, however so is the current atmosphere you find yourself in. If there is much depth and undoing resolved in a retreat that focuses 100% on this, there will still be an integration process of continuing this whole work in daily active life upon return. If you start to integrate this work in daily active life now, and in your current living situation, then you will build up enough steam and can end up in manifested Union in God's time surely. Then if you decided to come to a retreat or even do your own retreat, the steam from the practice in active life, will be compounded and deepen even more in a retreat setting.

Your original premise in your question is basically an Egoic excuse, self justification, and a resistance towards starting. It is silly and should be let go of, and see how that excuse is coming from the ego, something that isn't even you. So there is a choice of either believing it and living with that resistance, or not believing it and starting the whole process regardless of the excuses that ego constructs.

In daily life, every single situation or what I call micro event, is an opportunity to see how the ego is constructing itself and how it's filtering reality. That then allows you a chance to see it, be aware of it, be conscious of it, and to see how silly its constructs are. Those constructs are imagined and daydreamt illusions that if seen through as unreal, fall away and are no longer identified with.

These daily micro event situations can't be reconstructed at retreat. However, the retreat atmosphere can be reconstructed in your daily life by setting aside the time to dive back into the No Self Atmosphere in passive and silent settings.

Question: Wow, these exchanges are amazing! So what you're basically saying is let go of any views so that you no longer have any views am I right?

Answer: Yes, it's the cultivation of not having any views, along with not having the view of cultivating anything (no views). Technically, there's nothing wrong with having a view or an opinion or a laugh or thoughts or so forth, but we are not clinging to anything or any views. It's that view that 'I am this body, I am the thinker of thoughts' that is what blocks access to Union. When that's no longer believed in and let go of, it really starts to open up the nakedness of experience, and that's how Union will manifest, when that nakedness is in place and is deeply surrendered into and accepted.

Also, the thinker of thoughts, is itself just a thought, just a belief, and ultimately unreal.

It sounds like you've had a direct insight into this whole process, however letting go of any and all views is just one part of many. There's a lot more to all of this than just letting go of all views and to even get to that point, you have to first become aware of the views as they arise in the mind. If there's no awareness of them, then we are living an unconscious life filtered by views. There's also seeing that the thought 'I' is just a thought, that everything is taking place prior to and not limited to what you think of it. For example if I ask you to be aware of the chair your sitting on, you probably weren't aware of it until I mentioned something, which shows that 'sitting' was happening all on its own, regardless of your unconsciousness of it and was happening prior to whatever thoughts you had about it.

So we are getting to this nakedness of reality prior to our unconsciousness and our imagined labels. There's also surrender, love, flow, openness, and many more aspects and insights that eventually come to life in this process.

Question: You've brought up the idea of different types of Egoic constructs. Can you give me an example of what these consist of and how one is to work with them?

Answer: Egoic constructs consist of any role in life, and what the ego believes that role should ideally be about. Employee, business owner, boyfriend/girlfriend mother/father, sibling, marriage, priest/monk, teacher/student, success, failure, romance, gardener, poet, artist, writer, and the list goes on and on. It also covers psychological fragmentation in constructs based on seeing another person have something you don't, and desiring the same, keeping up with the joneses, grass greener on the other side, and so forth.

I'll be covering these in the next book extensively; however, the ego is programmed in such a way that it idealizes each of these roles in a certain set of filters based on illusions and worldly programs that have entered into our constructed belief systems based on culture, parents, media, peers, and so on.

So in your case for example, you know from experience that what you thought it would take to be a Mother was night and day compared to actually experiencing and playing out the motherly role. The Egoic idea of what being a Mother is all about is also filtered by self esteem, life circumstances, moods and emotions, biases, all of which differ and change throughout the passage of time.

What we're doing is letting go of the illusions of all and any roles and ideas about them, and just allowing a naked playing out of the tasks at hand when they need to be done. So the transition between waker upper, tooth brusher, breakfast chef, mother, employee, side business owner and all other roles are all stripped to a point of seeing everything as happening on its own.

Another example of Egoic constructs would be the 'I _____(Fill in the blank.)' There's the angry I, happy I, needy I, sad I, low self esteem I, hopeful I, ambitious I, hungry I, thirsty I, and so on. Depending on the time of day and surrounding circumstance, any one of these or a combination of these will be in place, filtering reality and dictating the way the illusions play out.

If it's hungry 'I' and someone calls you on the phone to ask you something, then there's a chance annoyed 'I' and impatient 'I' will filter the conversation in such as way so as to get the call over with as soon as possible in order to be able to eat. Each one of these is a construct, and yet each one of these is a habitually imagined and conditioned reaction that the ego identifies itself as.

However, it's really only the 'I' that needs to be deconstructed in order for everything else to fall away like a tipped over domino effect. This is the cool thing about going through with all of this during your regular life is that all the differing life situations will bring out all of these constructs to be seen and deconstructed. Applying the Blueprints to Union is an active deconstruction of the 'I-Thought' and all the Egoic constructs that come with it.

***

About the Author

A Christian Mystic Nondualist, Brother Dominick chooses not to live or be defined by any labels or concepts, choosing instead to be a simple Lover and Experiencer of God. Living both a normal active life in the world, he does so as a hidden hermit blending in with everyday regular activities of life, while also setting aside lengthy amounts of time for self retreats in solitude in various hermitages, retreat centers, and sometimes, just a tent in the woods.

After spending 14 months within the confines of Evangelical Christianity and an eventual re-Baptism, he was indwelled by the Holy Spirit and underwent a mystical death of the ego, what some denominations call, 'to be Slain by the Spirit." The Mystical indwelling of the Spirit activated within Dominick a number of higher spiritual faculties, known as gifts of the Spirit, including the peace that surpasses all understanding, transcendence, Holy detachment (sometimes referred to in Eastern Orthodoxy as Holy Dispassion), divine infused contemplation, blinded by the light of illumination, access to memories of our true origins, and a number of others. All of this eventually led to a lengthy period and passage through the Dark Night of the Soul, and it was during this period that he would be introduced to a Christian Mystic Hermit from South Africa, who would help him traverse the Dark Night by surrendering fully to it and furthering the death and disidentification of any ego remnants.

After the Dark Night, Union with God would occur along with deeper depths of inner revelation leading to a collapse of all identifications and a surrendered life in the ever present totality of Union's Omnipresence on a number of different levels that to this day, continue to flower, evolve, reveal, and grow in a never ending learning process where life is the teacher.

Dominick holds biannual retreats in several North American states and travels globally to make guest appearances in retreats put together by students and friends. Because there is no judgment and divisions in his experiences, he is approached by people from a variety of backgrounds, denominations, and even different religions, saying, "Just like Jesus did, I welcome everybody with Love and do not experience divisions or judgments of that person in Union and Love. Even though I continue to work with felons, abuse victims, atheists, agnostics, Buddhists, Natives,

Catholics, and people from a variety of backgrounds, I don't see them by their labels. There is just Love and openness with a willingness to show people how to access that which is already waiting within them to be expressed as Union."

Dominick is currently working on additional books such as Blueprints to Union 2 focusing on healing past traumas and deconstructing a list of dualities, a third book about detailed mechanics of the ego with the remedy of St. Francis of Assisi's quote: "What we are looking for, is what is looking," and a few others in the works.

www.BrotherDominick.org

***

Proof

Made in the USA
Charleston, SC
30 October 2016